CYBER-PHYSICAL ATTACK DEFENSES

Preventing Damage to Buildings and Utilities

By: Luis Ayala

About the Author

Luis Ayala worked over 25 years for the Department of Defense with the past 11 years at the Defense Intelligence Agency. Prior to his appointment as a Defense Intelligence Senior Leader in 2008, he held several leadership positions at the Branch and Division levels. His tenure culminated with the position as Senior Technical Expert (facilities/construction). Mr. Ayala earned his Bachelor of Architecture degree from Pratt Institute and he received his Master of Science and Technology Intelligence from the National Intelligence University. NIU is the Intelligence Community's sole accredited, federal degree granting institution. His Master's thesis titled *"Cybersecure Facilities for the Intelligence Community"* is classified.

Mr. Ayala was awarded the DIA Civilian Expeditionary Medal and the Civilian Combat Support Medal.

This book is dedicated to my wife, Paula. She has been and always will be my best friend, a wonderful wife and a great mother to our son Chris.

Luis Ayala

PREFACE

What is a cyber-physical attack? A cyber-physical attack is one in which a wholly digital attack against **Cyber-Physical Systems (CPS)** caused physical destruction of equipment. A *cyber-physical attack* is different from an *enterprise network cyber-attack* designed to steal money, exfiltrate information, or hold a computer hostage for ransom. Those attacks are fairly simple and can be carried out by a cyber-criminal, or even a garden variety **cracker** (NOTE: A *"cracker"* is a *hacker* with malicious intent. All *hackers* are NOT *crackers*. The terms are not interchangeable).

Cyber-Physical Systems are engineered systems that are built from, and depend upon, the seamless integration of computational algorithms and physical components. Traditional analysis tools are unable to cope with the full complexity of CPS or adequately predict system behavior. As the *Internet of Things (IoT)* scales to billions of connected devices - with the capacity to sense, control, and otherwise interact with the human and physical world - the requirements for dependability, security, safety, and privacy grow immensely. One barrier to progress is the lack of appropriate science and technology to conceptualize and design for the deep interdependencies among engineered systems and the natural world.

Hacking into a *Building Controls Systems (BCS), Industrial Controls Systems (ICS)*, and *Supervisory Controls and Data Acquisition (SCADA)* networks is not the same as breaking into enterprise networks that process information. *BCS, ICS* and *SCADA* systems are much more complex. Breaking into a controls system is only a means to an end. The target is not the network itself, it is the equipment being controlled.

A *cyber-physical attack* represents a **weaponization** of the Internet.

Although designing a <u>catastrophic</u> *cyber-physical attack* scenario to exploit a particular physical process requires a solid engineering background and in-depth *destructive* knowledge of the target controls system (**Cyber-Physical Attack Engineering**)---you don't need an engineering background to figure out how to turn equipment off.

i

In addition, a typical *ICS* contains multiple *control loops* and sometimes the *control loops* are *nested* and/or *cascading*, so the *set point* for one loop is based on the *process variable* output from *another loop*. Interrupting one process can have a ripple effect through the factory. *Supervisory control loops* and *lower-level loops* operate continuously over the duration of a process with cycle times of milliseconds.

A *cracker* doesn't need to have an engineering degree to figure out that a large change in the *setpoint* (or process values) on a proportional feedback system will have a larger effect than a small change that would be tolerated based on the sensitivity of the control system and the process. But, even a small change that results in sluggish response in the short-term could have a major effect over a relatively long period of time.

The only saving grace is that a *newbie* or *script kiddie* will not thoroughly understand complex manufacturing processes. While a *newbie* may be able to turn off the lights in the factory, I doubt he would know how to increase the *deadband* (an interval of a signal domain where no action occurs - the system is 'dead' - i.e. the output is zero) on *voltage regulators*, or cause repeated *activation-deactivation cycles*.

Hacking a chemical plant to create a weapon of mass destruction (a Bhopal-style catastrophic failure) for example, requires knowledge of physics, chemistry and engineering, as well as a great deal about how the network is laid out, and a keen understanding of *process-aware defensive systems*. The most a *newbie* could hope to do is to turn something off.

A well-qualified attacker (such as a foreign security service) hitting a building or utilities controls network seeks to take control over the equipment. Those *crackers* understand the equipment they will be controlling. No offense but, most *IT guys* are not familiar with electrical and mechanical equipment, industrial and manufacturing equipment, or utility equipment, so they wouldn't know how to defend them. That's because they don't know the equipment or processes being controlled.

The same is true of the folks in charge of physical security at these facilities. The typical *security guys* don't know anything about electrical and mechanical systems, or how computer networks are designed. Let's face it, they don't have the budget or the training to deal with these new threats.

The owner is looking to the facility guys, the IT guys and the security guys to work together to defend their physical plant, and in many cases, these guys aren't even talking to each other. Most of the time, they think cyber-physical security is someone else's responsibility! In essence, "**nobody is minding the store**". An effective defense against *cyber-physical attacks* requires **procedural safeguards**, such as frequent password changes, equipment inspections, random drills, security awareness programs, records retention programs, etc.

So, what is the big deal?

On December 3 1984, in Bhopal, India there was an *industrial accident* at a pesticide plant that immediately killed *at least 3,800 people* and caused significant morbidity and premature death for many thousands more. That was only one incident with a release of only 40 tons of methyl isocyanate gas. Of course, this was an accident and not a cyber-physical attack, but it should give you an idea what could happen in a worst-case scenario.

Imagine you wake up in the morning and go the bathroom. You turn on the faucet and nothing happens. You go back to the bedroom and the clock is flashing 12:00. You hit the power button on the TV remote and nothing happens. It's a little warm in the house but the air conditioning doesn't work. Then you realize that though the sun is out and it's a normal weekday, you don't hear any cars going by. You go outside to your car and it won't start – even the radio doesn't work. The cell phone has no signal and won't stay on when you power up. The toaster doesn't heat up and you have to light the gas stove with a match. It's a nice day so you walk to work and notice a line outside the supermarket, but the doors are locked. You ask why they don't open up and they say there is no power to run the cash registers. Even their backup generator won't start. None of the traffic lights work, but there are no cars on the road anyway. This is a *cyber-physical attack* that affects all utilities, and many electronic devices.

Or, imagine you've been waiting for months to find a kidney donor and the day you go in for a kidney transplant, the hospital is attacked and the refrigeration equipment that holds human organs is hacked. A malicious attacker changed the temperature setting of the refrigerators overnight, or cut the power entirely. All human organs were lost. Yes, these systems are designed with alarms that send messages to beepers and email, but a determined attacker can defeat those alarms.

Another example is what actually happened at a Chrysler assembly plant. An attacker shut down one auto plant with a worm that quickly spread to all other Chrysler plants, idling 50,000 workers. These were professionally-installed *industrial control networks* with firewalls and safety features. I suspect they were protected in much the same way that many enterprise networks are protected today.

The bad news is that *crackers* are getting better at what they do. In the good old days, an attacker would use a virus or worm to take over your computer. Nowadays they can attack your computer without loading any files at all. That's because all the files they need to take over are already loaded on your computer. That's called a **Fileless Cyber-Attack**. All they need to do is trick you into giving them permission to access those files. Anti-virus software has gotten very good at detecting and stopping a computer virus. Attackers find it much easier to fool a human using *social engineering*.

In order for you to begin to understand what is going through the mind of someone trying to break into your computer network, I include a lot of **Hackerspeak**, or **Leet-speak** in this book. See the definitions a little further on. This should give you some insight into the mind of a *hacker*.

This book was written to help Owners, Architects, Engineers, and facilities and infrastructure maintenance personnel understand the vulnerability of SCADA systems, building controls systems, and industrial controls systems to cyber-physical attack. The book includes simple descriptions of the vulnerabilities (attack vectors) of automated equipment controls common to buildings, industry and utilities. The book also lists the different types of *cyber-physical attacks* discovered. It is a handy desk reference for Architects, Engineers, Building Managers, Students, Researchers and Consultants interested in preventing cyber-physical attacks. Please read the definitions of a "*hacker*" and a "*cracker*" and stop referring to *hackers* as bad guys. Thanx

The price of connectivity is less security. The more connected a device is, the less secure it will be.

If there is only one thing you get out of this book, it should be this:

Building Controls Systems and SCADA systems should not be connected to the Internet – unless the intended purpose is to have them hacked and out of action.

Other cybersecurity books I've written are available at: www.Amazon.com.

- Cybersecurity Lexicon

- Cybersecurity for Hospitals and Healthcare Facilities: A Guide to Detection and Prevention

- Cyber-Physical Attack Recovery Procedures: A Step-by-Step Preparation and Response Guide

Rather than repeat much of the jargon used by engineers and cybersecurity folks here, this book contains definitions not found in the *Cybersecurity Lexicon*. Otherwise this book would be twice the number of pages. If you see a word that's unfamiliar here, please refer to the *Cybersecurity Lexicon*.

Contents

.

PREVENTING CYBER-PHYSICAL ATTACKS

Perfect cyber-security is unachievable, and probably unaffordable. However, there are steps you can take to reduce the risk of *cyber-physical attack* against buildings, manufacturing facilities and utilities.

1. Physical Access to the Hardware

Let me begin by saying that unless you implement stringent physical access controls, the rest of what I am about to tell you will be in vain. Cyber assets and their communication media should be protected 100% of the time with a six-wall border to limit physical tampering with the systems and media. Not only should access doors have locks, the doors should automatically close. Do not allow employees to prop doors open for any reason.

An attacker begins by *Footprinting* the target facility. He sifts through *open-source* material found on the Internet to learn all he can about the target, including who works there, what equipment is there, and where it is located. An attacker may visit the building, sniff the wireless spectrum, look in dumpsters, and use *social engineering* to assemble a very good picture of the target network and its equipment to determine where the vulnerabilities are.

Ofttimes, I've been able to wander into a *Building Control Center* without being challenged. All I need is a construction helmet and a clip board. In fact, there are professional *hackers* called **Sneakers** that specialize in finding ways to penetrate a physical security barrier.

> **Sneaker** - *Hackerspeak* referring to an individual hired to break into physical places in order to test their security, usually using *social engineering*.

To compound the problem, most of the time people sitting at a workstation connected to the BCS network don't even log out when they leave the room. Anyone can sit at the workstation and sabotage the equipment when the user steps out. A visitor wishing to compromise network security need only plug a **Rubber Ducky**, **LAN Turtle** or **Bash Bunny** into a USB port and the system is "*pwned*".

Rubber Ducky - *A Keystroke Injection Attack Platform* hidden in a USB thumb drive. Whether it be a Windows, Mac, Linux or Android device, any *USB* device claiming to be a *Keyboard HID* will be automatically detected and accepted by most modern operating systems. By taking advantage of this inherent trust with scripted keystrokes (at speeds beyond 1000 words per minute), traditional countermeasures can be bypassed.

LAN Turtle - A covert *Penetration Testing* tool providing *stealth remote access, network intelligence gathering, and man-in-the-middle* surveillance capabilities through a simple graphic shell. A *cracker* can use this to:
- Scan the network using nmap
- DNS Spoof clients to phishing sites
- Exfiltrate data via SSHFS
- Access the entire LAN through a site-to-site *VPN* with the *LAN Turtle* acting as gateway

Bash Bunny - A *USB drive* that emulates combinations of trusted USB devices — like *gigabit Ethernet, serial, flash storage* and *keyboards* so computers are tricked into divulging data, exfiltrating documents, installing backdoors and many more *exploits*. Slide the switch to your payload of choice, plug the *Bash Bunny* into the victim computer and watch the multi-color LED. With a quad-core CPU and desktop-class SSD it goes from *plug to pwn* in 7 seconds.

If the attacker has lots of time, he can install a ***Throwing Star LAN Tap***.

LAN Tap - A *passive Ethernet tap*, requiring no power for operation. To the target network, the LAN Tap looks just like a section of cable, but the wires in the cable extend to the monitoring ports in addition to connecting one target port to the other. The *Throwing Star LAN Tap's* monitoring ports (J3 and J4) are receive-only; they connect to the receive data lines on the monitoring station, but do not connect to the network's transmit lines. This makes it impossible for the monitoring station to accidentally transmit data packets onto the target network.

If the attacker has to work quickly, he can insert a **Ralink** into a USB port in the back of a computer. That would turn the computer into a wide-open *backdoor* to the network, with little chance of being discovered.

Ralink - An incredibly small USB Wi-Fi adapter. These are nearly impossible to spot unless you are looking for them. Also, some USB ports are <u>inside</u> the computer case.

If the attacker has lots of time and needs longer range, he can plug a **Wi-Fi Pineapple** into any USB port. It's so small it's not that difficult to hide. It would be tough to spot-unless someone knows it shouldn't be there,

Wi-Fi Pineapple - An advanced wireless device used for *penetration testing* or used by *crackers* as a *rogue access point* for *reconnaissance, man-in-the-middle, tracking, logging* and *reporting*. Not only would the attacker be able to collect/monitor data, he would also be able to modify control **setpoints**. It provides a common interface to wireless sensors and switches. These are not secure and are easily compromised by any garden-variety *cracker*, junior-grade.

For short range communications, a *cracker* can install a **Ubertooth One.** These are a little larger, so are easier to spot – if you are looking for them.

Ubertooth One - An opensource *Bluetooth* test tool from Michael Ossmann. An affordable platform that can be used for *Bluetooth monitoring*. Also used for the development of new *Bluetooth* and wireless technologies.

Be on the lookout for a **Keystroke Logger Attack.** A program or USB device designed to record which keys are pressed on a computer keyboard used to obtain passwords or encryption keys and thus bypass other security measures. A **Mouse Logger** works much the same way.

Any of these tools will allow a *cracker* to alter *setpoints* to raise the limits outside the intended design parameters of the equipment manufacturer. A **Setpoint** (also *set point*) is the desired or target value for an essential variable of a system to describe a standard configuration or norm for the system. For example, a boiler might have a *temperature setpoint*, which is the temperature the boiler control system aims to maintain. This attack is called a **Setpoint Override.**

Most *setpoint* loads in a heating system operate year-round at temperatures above the reset operating temperature. When the *setpoint* load requires heat, this overrides the *Warm Weather Shut Down and Reset* temperature of the control. This function allows the heating system to operate only at the temperature required to satisfy the current load.

End points (CD-ROM, USB, RJ-45, RS-232, RS-485, LON connectors, terminal block connections, serial and parallel ports, jacks, plugs, etc.) should be <u>monitored</u> for security state, attempted access violations, malicious behavior and vulnerabilities. Install *end point protections* on the servers, control consoles and all IP-enabled devices to prevent *Stuxnet*-like intrusion from *insiders* purposefully or haplessly installing *malware* from USB drives (or from installing external attack code that made it onto the BCS network).

Detection devices should be used to identify any attempt to setup *rogue communication devices*, new systems, connectivity, applications and wireless access. Maintain a list of *approved BCS devices* and the connectivity and communication profiles between devices.

Enforce strict controls and *separation of duties* for direct access and monitoring of control room operators, administrators and others with direct access. I recommend you implement the **Two-Person Control** whenever possible.

> **Two-Person Control -** Continuous surveillance and control of positive control material at all times by a minimum of two authorized individuals, each capable of detecting incorrect and unauthorized procedures with respect to the task being performed and each familiar with established security and safety requirements.
>
> **Two-Person Integrity -** System of storage and handling designed to prohibit individual access by requiring the presence of at least two authorized individuals, each capable of detecting incorrect or unauthorized security procedures with respect to the task being performed. See *no-lone zone.*

Enforce limits on access and hold individuals accountable for their actions. Do not ignore security policy rule violations. Ensure employees are only granted the least privileges necessary to do their jobs. The security objective of **Least Privilege** is to grant users only the access they need to perform their official duties. Studies have shown that in 2016, 47 percent of analyzed organizations had at least 1,000 sensitive files open to every employee; and 22 percent had 12,000 sensitive files open to every employee.

Equipment vendors will want to bring along a laptop to plug into your BCS system to check the performance of their equipment. Again, this is for their convenience and will degrade your security. Do not allow a vendor to connect his laptop computer to the BCS unless absolutely necessary.

If you must, let them use your laptop and test their programs by use of a **sandbox** on a test network (**Digital Twin**). A sandbox is a security mechanism to execute untested or untrusted programs or code, from unverified or untrusted third parties, suppliers, users or websites, without risking harm to the BCS network. A *sandbox* provides a tightly controlled set of resources for guest programs to run in (not a virtual host, separate network). Network access, the ability to inspect the host system or read from input devices are NEVER allowed and ALWAYS heavily restricted.

Make sure every laptop computer gets a thorough cleaning and is scanned before and after use for *malware* and *spyware.*

Do not permit wireless control of devices by anyone from inside or outside the building. Whenever possible, use *point-to-point* connections. This includes your own employees. This is a vulnerability that can open all kinds of doors. Keep *smart phones* out of secure areas, except in an emergency.

Today, most *smartphones* from Verizon Wireless have a built-in **mobile hotspot** function—allowing you to access the Internet anytime. A laptop can also be set up as a *mobile hot spot.*

The point here is that there are many ways to compromise a Building Controls System if you have *physical access* to the hardware. There are many, many access points already on site. A hospital is probably the most vulnerable because every patient room has a *network access point* that anybody can plug into.

Some *cyber-physical attacks* cannot be carried out without access to the physical hardware on site. So, why make it easier for an attacker by leaving the doors unlocked? In fact, you even need to secure your trash bins because *crackers* have been known to resort to **Dumpster Diving.**

Dumpster Diving - Obtaining passwords and organization's directories by searching through discarded trash bin. Also, referred to as *"skipping."*

Common Sense Physical Security Tips:

- Provide lockable rooms or locking enclosures for all system components (e.g., servers, clients, and networking hardware) and for the systems used to manage and control physical access (e.g., servers, lock controllers, and alarm control panels).
- Provide a method for *tamper detection* on lockable or locking enclosures.
- Change locks, locking codes, keycards, and any other keyed entrances when after any building construction or renovation.
- Reprogram codes (e.g., remove default codes) on locks and locking devices so that the codes/passwords are unique and do not repeat codes used in the past.
- Install network cabling that is routed thru unprotected areas only in metal conduit (that can be visually inspected easily).
- Provide *two-factor authentication* for physical access control.

- Have the BCS equipment supplier certify and provide documentation that communication channels are as direct as possible (e.g., communication paths between devices in one network security zone do not pass through devices maintained at a low security level or cross unnecessarily into low security zones).
- Remove or disable all services and ports not required for normal operation, emergency operations, or troubleshooting. This includes communication ports and physical input/output ports (e.g., USB docking ports, CD/DVD drives, video ports, and serial ports). Inventory and document disabled ports, connectors, and interfaces.
- Install an Uninterruptable Power Supply for all computer equipment.
- Set the BIOS to only boot from the C drive.

2. Internet Access

Most company's Building Controls Systems (BCS) are connected to the Internet in one way or another. Sometimes, the owner *thinks* the BCS is not connected because the network diagram doesn't show any connections. What the owner doesn't know is that over the years, vendors installed *rogue access points* so they can monitor performance of their equipment remotely. Unfortunately, the owner has lost control of the network security without even knowing they are vulnerable.

Other times, somebody installed a *printer* on the network without knowing it has a *wireless card* in it (or *fax*). They didn't ask for wireless printing capability, so they are unaware that it defaulted to "On" when the printer was installed (or when the power goes off) so the *default password* (usually "password") was never changed. An attacker searching for vulnerabilities will easily detect the wireless printer and use that opening to attack the BCS network.

Some equipment is too critical to ever be connected to a network. Anesthesia equipment or surgical robots are two examples. Of course, the equipment vendor will tell you he has a *"magic box"* that cannot be hacked. **Don't believe it**. Anything can be hacked. Salesmen promise the Earth, Moon and Stars – but all they deliver is *rocks*.

Commercial organizations have been alarmed to discover through searches for internet connected devices on **SHODAN, Censys** and **ZoomEye** that their BCS network is indeed accessible over the Internet – despite assurances to the contrary. Such a discovery counteracts the pervasive folk-myth of *security by obscurity* and even *air-gap* systems are vulnerable.

SHODAN - *SHODAN* is a search engine that lets a user find specific types of computers (routers, servers, etc.) connected to the internet using a variety of filters. This can be information about the server software, what options the service supports, a welcome message or anything else that the client can find out before interacting with the server. *SHODAN* searches the Internet for publicly accessible devices, concentrating on *SCADA* systems. If your building control system is listed on *SHODAN*, it probably has been hacked. *SHODAN* will reveal a device's fingerprint, key exchange (kex) algorithms, server host key algorithms, encryption algorithms, MAC algorithms, and compression algorithms. One of the most popular searches is *"default password."*

Again, one of the most popular searches is "*default password*."

Censys - *Censys* is a search engine designed to search for *internet-connected devices*. It collects data using both *ZMap* and *ZGrab* (an application layer scanner that operates via *ZMap*), which in this case scan the IPV4 address space. Censys can perform full-text searches. Here are two sample searches:
https://www.censys.io/ipv4?q=80.http.get.status_code%3A%20200 – this allows you to search for all hosts with a specific *HTTP* status code. You can also just type in an IP address, such as: "66.24.206.155" or "71.20.34.200" (those are fake). To find hosts in 23.0.0.0/8 and 8.8.8.0/24, type in "23.0.0.0/8 or 8.8.8.0/24."

ZoomEye - ZoomEye is a Chinese *search engine* similar to *SHODAN* that allows the user find specific network components. ZoomEye is *hacker-friendly* and uses *Xmap* and *Wmap* at its core for grabbing data from publicly exposed devices and web services (http://ics.zoomeye.org). ZoomEye allows you to search by:

- **Application name and version** number
- **Location**: **country** code (for example: UK, IT, ES, FR, CN, JP.) and name of **city**
- **Port** number
- **Name of the operating system** (for example os:linux)
- **Service name**
- **Hostname** (for example hostname:google.com)
- **IP address** (for example ip:8.8.8.8)
- **CIDR segment** (for example cidr:8.8.8.8/24)
- **Domain name** (for example site:google.com)
- **Headers** in HTTP request
- **SEO keywords** defined inside <meta name="Keywords">
- **Description** inside <meta name="description">
- **Title** inside <title>
- **Apache httpd** – finds results for *Apache* http servers
- **device:"webcam"** – finds a list of webcams with an internet connection

Once the *cracker* knows what software applications are running on the target network, he can develop a specific set of tools to *exploit known vulnerabilities*. For example, say the *cracker* learns the building controls system at a target hospital is *Siemens* SIMATIC STEP 7 TIA (Portal). In February 2015, *Siemens* reported two vulnerabilities on that software. One vulnerability would allow a successful *man-in-the-middle attack* remotely. The other will allow a *cracker* with local access to reconstruct *protection-level passwords*. A *Siemens* software update is available, but has not been installed at all hospitals.

Of course, if the network is connected to the Internet, then the *cracker* can get in easily. I don't care how many assurances you get from equipment vendors that their "*magic box*" is impenetrable. *If your network is connected to the Internet, it ~~can~~ will be hacked.* In fact, if it is connected to the Internet, I can say with a lot of confidence that it *has already been sniffed, hacked* and *mapped*. I would be surprised if you don't already have *spyware* and a number of *backdoors* already installed on your BCS network.

My recommendation is for you to bring in a third-party company to perform a **Penetration Test** and a **Vulnerability Test** to make sure your BCS is not connected to the Internet. *Do not rely on a vendor that sells you equipment for your BCS to pentest your network.* Hackers sometimes call these experts **Samurai.** That's *Hackerspeak* for a hacker who hires out for legal cracking jobs (an electronic locksmith). I highly recommend you have these tests performed frequently, and not necessarily advertise when the tests will be performed – even to your own line employees (more on that later).

A *penetration test* is a test performed by an *ethical hacker* to determine system vulnerability. *Pen-testing* is not the same as *vulnerability testing*. The intent of *vulnerability testing* is just to identify potential problems, but *pen-testing* is designed to *attack* those problems. The tools used for *pen-testing* can be classified into two kinds – *scanners* and *attackers*. This is because *pen-testing* is exploiting the weak spots. There are some software/tools that will only show you the weak spots, some that show *and* attack.

Making sure the BCS is not connected to the Internet may sound easy, but it isn't. Sometimes the BCS is designed to feed information to the company enterprise network. The problem is the enterprise network *is* connected to the Internet. An attacker that can hack into an enterprise network will use that as a gateway to hack into the BCS.

A good *Pentest* company (such as ***FoxGuard Solutions***) will use a number of tools. **Nessus** is one of the most robust vulnerability identifier tools available. *Nessus* specializes in compliance checks, IP scans, sensitive data searches, and website scanning and aids in finding the 'weak-spots'. Another tool is **PunkSPIDER.** *PunkSPIDER* is a global web application vulnerability *search engine*. The driving force behind it is ***PunkSCAN***, a security scanner that can execute a massive number of security scans all at once. Among the types of attacks that *PunkSPIDER* can search for include *Cross-Site Scripting* (XSS), *Blind SQL Injection* (BSQLI), *Operating System Command Injection* (OSCI), and *Path Traversal* (TRAV).

Some equipment vendors will insist they need remote access to your BCS. Do not permit remote access to the BCS from *outside or inside* the building by anyone (maintain the air gap). This access is for *their* convenience and will degrade *your* security. Remember, if a device has an IP Address – it can be hacked. It's bad enough that all your BCS networks have already been mapped by *crackers*, let's not make it easy for them to get in.

3. Disable Everything You Don't Need

When purchasing new BCS equipment, include language in the Request for Proposal (RFP) requiring the vendor to remove all unnecessary software, disable unused ports and install the latest software patches before you accept the work and that new patches/fixes are implemented when they are released. The vendor must certify in writing that the equipment complies with all the requirements in the RFP – regardless whatever weasel words they sneak into their proposal.

Require the vendor to change all default passwords and set appropriately secure login credentials. Do not purchase equipment with hard-wired default passwords that YOU cannot change. The most common configuration problem is credentials management (i.e., weak passwords, shared user accounts and insufficiently protected credentials), followed by weak or non-existent firewall rules and network design weaknesses.

Control access to trusted devices. For example, for access to a segmented network, use a bastion host with access control lists (ACLs) for ingress/egress access. Never place a computer or a monitor where they can be seen by outsiders (such as facing a window) where a specially-designed aerial hacker drone can monitor the network such as a **scanner hack**.

Scanner Hack - Researchers in Israel have shown off a novel technique that would allow attackers to wirelessly command devices using a laser light, bypassing so-called *air gaps*. Firewalls and *intrusion detection systems* can block communication going to and from suspicious domains and IP addresses over the Internet. To bypass normal detection methods, researchers in Israel were able to use a **laser-equipped aerial drone** to communicate covertly with *malware*. The technique uses a **flatbed scanner** as the gateway through which an attacker can send commands to their malware on a victim's network. The attack would also work by hijacking an existing light source installed near the scanner, such as a "smart" lightbulb. The attack could be used against industrial control systems to shut down processes on "air gapped" networks, which aren't directly connected to the internet.

In order to reduce the number of threat vectors, you should <u>remove</u> or <u>disable</u> any unnecessary applications or capabilities. Better to <u>remove</u> than disable something that can later be enabled without your knowledge. Disable unused ports as well as remote protocols that are insecure (like Telnet). Disable all protocols that communicate inbound to your trusted resources that are not critical to functionality.

Maintain the *air-gap* of your BCS networks at all costs. **Air Gap** computers are physically isolated from unsecured computer networks, such as the public Internet or an unsecured local area network for security purposes. Air gap computers are not connected by wire or wirelessly and (generally) cannot communicate directly with each other. Rely on the **Ten-Finger Interface**.

> **Ten-Finger Interface** - *Hackerspeak* referring to the air gap between two networks that cannot be directly connected for security reasons; interface is achieved by placing two terminals side by side and having an operator read from one and type into the other.

eMail is the *cracker*'s preferred method of gaining access to any network that has Internet access. **NEVER** allow email access on the **Process Network or the Control Network**. Employees should have a separate computer for email, preferably not in the same room as the BCS servers. Don't even install *Microsoft Office* on BCS workstations. The *process network* usually hosts the *SCADA* servers and *human-machine interfaces*. The *control network* hosts all the devices on one side that controls the actuators and sensors of the physical layer, and on the other side provide the control interface to the *process network*.

Financially-motivated *cyber-criminals* are now launching tailored, victim-specific *spear-phishing* campaigns. These *crackers* are targeting a large number of organizations and they quickly shift *tools, tactics, and procedures* (TTPs). In years past, cyber-crime was frequently opportunistic. Today, *cyber-criminals* are exhibiting unusual persistence using tools developed by *advanced persistent threat* (APT) actors and are attempting to re-compromise an organization after remediation.

A *cracker* typically will send an email containing *Active Content* (carries out or triggers actions automatically without the intervention of a user) such as a *Remote Access Trojan* (RAT) to an employee such as a building maintenance technician. I suggest you provide basic personal *cyber-hygiene training* to the entire workforce. I guarantee that will prevent <u>most</u> cyber-attacks because **91%** of successful data breaches started with a *spear-phishing attack.*

Also, do not enable web surfing from workstations on critical networks. If you already disconnected critical networks from the Internet, that is not a problem, I'm just saying. Perhaps, install one Internet-connected computer as **a kiosk** where employees can check email or surf the web. Heck, everybody has a smart phone anyway, so they don't need to access the Internet on their desktop computer.

If the only thing you get out of this is to **separate email traffic and web surfing from critical networks**, I will be happy.

Another thing, when you buy new equipment and remove a computer or server from your network, take out the hard drives and have them chopped up. Even erasing the data with a large magnet is not enough to ensure someone cannot retrieve the data once it's out of your hands.

I included some basic **Cyber-Hygiene** for email and USB stick **Do's and Don't**s in my book *"Cybersecurity for Hospitals and Healthcare Facilities."* That book also includes tips on creating strong passwords as well as example phishing text used by *crackers.* (Do you really think somebody in Africa is gonna wire you some money if you click on that attachment?)

4. Eliminate Common BCS Vulnerabilities

Key automation and control devices should be grouped into zones that share common security-level requirements. Utilize network segmentation to secure resources like VES systems, ICS, and devices. If you must have some connectivity, install a **DMZ**. If it were me, however, I wouldn't even trust that.

> **Demilitarized Zone (DMZ)** - An interface on a routing firewall that is similar to the interfaces found on the firewall's protected side. Traffic moving between the DMZ and other interfaces on the protected side of the firewall still goes through the firewall and can have firewall protection policies applied. It is a physical or logical subnetwork that contains and exposes the external-facing services (email, Web and Domain Name System servers) to an untrusted network. And, as far as I am concerned, all outside networks are untrusted.

Require user name/password combinations for all systems, including those that are not deemed "trustworthy." At a minimum, require vendor implement two-factor authentication on all trusted systems for any user account. If it were me, I would implement **3 Level Password Protection.** Requiring an additional password to authorize critical operations greatly reduces the surface area to attack the secondary credentials since they are used less often. For example: a *power-on* password, a *parameter setting* password, and a *parameter correction* password. Requiring re-authentication to perform special actions can protect against **Cross-Site Request Forgery** (CSRF) attacks. CSRF is also known as *one-click attack* or *session riding*.

I recommend you change passwords frequently, and sometimes with no-notice. Do not rely on employees to develop passwords because password attack software takes advantage of the fact that people tend to use uppercase characters at the start of passwords and numbers at the end. I recommend use of an **Automated Password Generator.** This uses an algorithm which creates random passwords that have no association with a particular user. It is also more effective against a **Dictionary Attack** and a **Brute Force Attack**.

Be on the lookout for a misconfigured and unencrypted router, which could potentially provide a gateway for *crackers*. Also, don't use a weak and outmoded form of encryption such as *WEP*.

Dictionary Attack - A dictionary attack takes place when an attacker utilizes a dictionary in an attempt to crack a password. Essentially, words from the dictionary are inputted into the password field to try to guess the password. Programs and tools exist that allow hackers to easily try various combinations of words in the dictionary against a user's password.

Brute-Force Attack - This type of cyber-attack is typically used as an end-all method to crack a difficult password. A brute-force attack is executed when an attacker tries to use all possible combinations of letters, numbers, and symbols to enter a correct password. Programs exist that help a *cracker* achieve this, such as **Zip Password Cracker Pro**. Any password can be cracked using the brute-force method, but it can take a very long time. The longer and more intricate a password is, the longer it will take a computer to try all of the possible combinations. **Cain & Abel** is a tool for cracking **encrypted passwords** or network keys.

I recommend you collect and aggregate the data related to login failures from all the hosts to check for *doorknob-rattling*. A **Doorknob-Rattling Attack** is when a *cracker* attempts a very few common username and password combinations on several computers resulting in very few failed login attempts.

A robust password management system is not enough for critical systems. Here, I recommend **Multi-Factor Authentication**. This is a method of computer access control in which a user is granted access only after successfully presenting several separate pieces of evidence to an authentication mechanism – typically at least two of the following categories: knowledge (password you know), possession (something you have), and biometrics (who you are). **Two-Factor Authentication** (also known as **2FA**) is a combination of *two* different components.

A word of caution about two-factor authentication when an SMS message is sent to a smart phone. NIST is no longer recommending solutions that use SMS because they may be vulnerable to **SS7 Cyber-Attacks**. SS7 (Signaling System 7) is a set of telephony signaling protocols used for data-roaming with vulnerabilities that allow attackers to listen to calls, intercept text messages, and pinpoint a device's location armed with just the target's phone number. Anyone can purchase SS7 access and send a routing request to direct a target's SMS-based text messages to another device, and, in the case of the bank accounts, steal any codes needed to login or greenlight money transfers (after the hackers obtained victim passwords).

I would also be leery of **One-Time Passwords.** A one-time password is a code issued by a small electronic device every 30 or 60 seconds that is valid for only one login session or transaction. Online thieves have created real-time *Trojan horse* programs that can issue transactions to a bank while the account holder is online, turning the one-time password into *a huge vulnerability.*

You may want to consider **Time-Dependent Passwords**. These are passwords that are valid only at a certain time of day or during a specified interval of time. The password for someone who normally works days would not work after hours, and vice versa. This would also help defend against a **Verifier Impersonation Attack.** This is an attack where the attacker impersonates the verifier in an authentication protocol, and somehow obtains another user's password (for example by **Shoulder Surfing**).

I recommend using a **Shadow Password File.** This is a building control system file in which encrypted user passwords are stored so that they aren't available to people who try to break into the building controls system. Also, make sure you keep **Escrow Passwords** in a *locked* safe. These are passwords that are written down and stored in a secure location that are used by emergency personnel when privileged personnel are unavailable.

Never store passwords in the open (unencrypted). Some searches on **GoogleDiggity** (a traditional Google hacking tool) can even retrieve the username and password list from *Microsoft FrontPage* servers.

Whenever possible, use **application layer encryption** (to avoid sensitive information being logged), end-to-end encryption, and encrypt files stored on hosts and servers. Network activity logs should always be encrypted. SSL is neither a network layer protocol nor an application layer protocol. It is one that "sits" between both layers.

Use real-time *anti-malware* protection and real-time *network scanning* locally on trusted hosts and where applicable. Rely on **Real-Time Protection** that immediately detects malware before it can do any harm by blocking or suspending malicious processes and infected files that try to start or connect to your system, effectively preventing malware from damaging your network and files. Use real-time registry protection to detect attempted registry changes. Use a program that alerts you when a program tries to make changes to your *registry*.

Develop a threat modeling system. Understand who's attacking you and why. There is a big difference between the ability of a garden-variety *script kiddie* and a *state-sponsored* organization bent on interfering with critical infrastructure. Designing an attack scenario to exploit a particular physical process requires a solid engineering background and in-depth *destructive* knowledge of the target SCADA system (**Cyber-Physical Attack Engineering**). Hacking a chemical plant, for example, requires knowledge of physics, chemistry and engineering, as well as a great deal about how the network is laid out, and a keen understanding of process-aware defensive systems. This represents a high (but not insurmountable) barrier to entry to garden-variety *script kiddies*, but is not a major obstacle for a *foreign intelligence service*.

Your company or utility may be a purely commercial enterprise, but be advised that military installations rely on public utilities, just like everyone else. <u>All victims are not necessarily the targets</u>. An attack on a company that provides vital utilities will be targeted in time of **Cyberwar.** These are actions by a nation-state to penetrate another nation's computers or networks for the purposes of causing damage or disruption. *Cyberwarfare* involves the use and targeting of computers and networks in warfare between nations or non-state actors, such as terrorist groups, political or ideological extremist groups, hacktivists, and transnational criminal organizations.

Keep in mind that *Foreign Policy Magazine* puts the size of China's *"hacker army"* at anywhere from 50,000 to 100,000 individuals. Although to date cyberwarfare has been limited to attacking information and communications networks, the possibility exists for cyber-attacks against computer-controlled equipment capable of causing harm and even death to a nation's civilian population.

5. Monitor All Activity on the BCS Network on a 24-hour Basis.

Inventory all direct and indirect trusts and associations (e.g., personnel, vendors, contractors, supply chain partners). This can be done by monitoring access (including physical access, when relevant) over time. Pay particular attention to those with too much privilege such as administrators, who should not have super access to the entire system contents or use shared passwords.

Improve logging in on trusted environments in addition to passing logs to *Security Information and Event Management* (SIEM) devices for third-party backup/analysis. Monitor systems and networks users are accessing over time for typical behavioral information between these trusts, their applications and their traffic. Assess and inventory all access to networks, systems and specific resources.

The system health of each cyber asset should be monitored for suspected system use of memory, CPU and number of network connections. Perform unscheduled, no-notice exercises to test network vulnerability to cyber-physical attack. Perform a periodic sweep (unannounced) of the area looking for **Rogue Access Points** and **Hidden Private Networks**.

Rogue Access Point - A rogue access point is a wireless access point that has been installed on a secure network without explicit authorization from a local network administrator, whether added by a well-meaning employee or by a malicious insider. Although it is technically easy for a well-meaning employee to install a "*soft access point*" or an inexpensive wireless router - perhaps to make access from mobile devices easier - it is likely that they will configure this as "open", or with poor security, and potentially allow access to unauthorized parties. If an attacker installs a rogue access point they are able to run various types of vulnerability scanners, and rather than having to be physically inside the building, a *cracker* can attack remotely - perhaps from a reception area, adjacent building, or car parking lot.

Snort is a network intrusion detection system that can detect probes or attacks and stealth port scans. A **stealth port scan** is designed to probe a server or host for *open ports* without being detected. The purpose is to identify services running on a host and exploit vulnerabilities.

> **Hidden Private Networks** can bypass the corporate network security. A computer that is being spied upon can be plugged into a legitimate corporate network that is heavy monitored for malware activity and at same time belongs to a private Wi-Fi network outside of the company network that is leaking confidential information off of an employee's computer. A computer like this is easily set up by a *double-agent* working in the IT department by installing a second wireless card in a computer. Using special software, he can remotely monitor an employee's computer through this second interface card without them being aware of a *side-band communication* channel pulling information off of his computer.

Use *intrusion detection* methods to look for attack signatures or anomalies that indicate a network attack may be in progress or may have already occurred. Use intrusion detection tools to *monitor transactions* at the *network layer* based on the source and destination addresses and protocol types and can look for "signatures" of known attack scenarios and anomalous behavioral patterns. Implement **Continuous Diagnostics and Mitigation (CDM).**

Scan the Wi-Fi spectrum at your site frequently looking for weak and open Wi-Fi networks, wireless printers without passwords, servers with outdated and vulnerable software, and unencrypted login pages to back-end databases. These are serious cyber-attack threat vectors.

Continuous Diagnostics and Mitigation is a dynamic approach to fortifying the cybersecurity of government networks and systems. CDM provides federal agencies with capabilities and tools that identify cybersecurity risks on an ongoing basis, prioritize these risks based upon potential impacts, and enable cybersecurity personnel to mitigate the most significant problems first. Agency-installed network sensors perform an automated search for known cyber flaws. Results feed into a local dashboard that produces customized reports, alerting network managers to their worst and most critical cyber risks based on standardized and weighted risk scores. Prioritized alerts enable agencies to efficiently allocate resources based on the severity of the risk. Progress reports track results, which can be used to compare security posture among department/agency networks. Summary information can feed into an enterprise-level dashboard to inform and situational awareness into cybersecurity risk posture across the federal government.

Use network vulnerability scanners to assess the configuration of the BCS network, identify security deficiencies and recommend countermeasures. Apply a *digital signature* to individual or combinations of event logs with sequence numbers to ensure that the event logs are complete.

Use sophisticated tools to automatically scan large amounts of data to analyze *event logs* and to present *suspicious events* to the auditor in a user-friendly manner.

Set up **Honeypots** and **Canaries**. These are "traps" to alert you when *crackers* are lurking in the shadows trying to hack your equipment. You can program setpoint traps, such as a specific temperature range for a certain area, to restrict override changes from going outside of set parameters and include PIN control on user access to system changes. You can also use a timed feature, to automatically revert to original settings after a temporary override period.

Honeypot - A system (e.g., a Web server) or system resource (e.g., a file on a server) that is designed to be attractive to potential *crackers* and intruders and has no authorized users other than its administrators.

Canary - Anything that can send up an observable alert if something happens. For example: you can set up a computer on a subnet such that no other computer should ever access that. If something touches it, you know it's outside normal behavior. Also, called a *tripwire*.

6. Monitor Insider (and Outsider) Behavior for Anomalies

Maintain workforce situational awareness and be on the lookout for **Insider Threats** such as counterproductive work behavior. This is defined as intentional behaviors that are contrary to legitimate organizational interests, including sabotage and espionage. The CERT Insider Threat Center includes a database of more than 850 cases of insider threats, including instances of fraud, theft and sabotage. Keep in mind that current access control systems that are designed to prevent the outsider threat.

Hospital Insider Threats - Insider threat to a hospital's critical infrastructure is more serious than outsider threats because an outside attacker is less likely to know the hospital's network vulnerabilities and its weaknesses as well as an insider would. The behavioral characteristics of hospital employees are potential indicators and patterns to detect insider threat activity. No one behavior by itself would be an issue, but questionable behaviors are more likely to be manifested in *multiple observables*. A list of observable employee behavior to look for which could serve as precursors to malicious activity can be found in my book *"Cybersecurity for Hospitals and Healthcare Facilities"*.

Watch for personal predispositions and stressors such as serious divorce, personal financial problems, mental health disorders, personality problems, social skills and decision-making biases, and *a history of rule conflicts* as *precursors of malicious events*. A financial sector report released in 2012 noted that 80% of the malicious acts were committed at work during working hours; 81% of the perpetrators planned their actions beforehand; 33% were described as "difficult" and 17% as being "disgruntled". Financial gain was a motive in 81% of cases, revenge in 23% of cases, and 27% of the people carrying out malicious acts were in financial difficulties at the time.

Avoid over-dependence on any insider (two-man rule). Address counterproductive work behavior consistently and fairly. Perceived variations in justice is a potential employee stressor. Perceived injustice is the most common cause of sabotage. **Do not ignore security policy rule violations.** Enforce limits on access and hold individuals accountable for their actions.

Monitoring insider behavior is particularly important when organization changes occur such as changes in management, organizational sanctions, or negative-workplace events (e.g., pay cut, missed promotion, below-average performance appraisal). Question anomalous behavior (why is insider working outside of normal working hours?). Watch for an insider **Tipping Point** (the *first observed event* at which an insider became disgruntled such as insider demoted, reprimanded for harassing coworker, or is being fired).

Insiders typically commit malicious acts *within 7 days of a tipping point*. Review the audit logs for actions or accesses that seem inappropriate. Reviews should be more frequent and extensive for individuals with higher privileges.

How much damage can an insider do?

Recently, a former contract security guard at a California company was found guilty of hacking his former employer, stealing proprietary software, and trashing the company network two weeks after he resigned his job. He had used an admin password to log into the company's payroll program and tampered with his overtime hours and work records. He gained access to the firm's network and stole archived emails, accounting software, and the databases used for accounting, invoices, and payroll operations. He also deleted or corrupted backup files and started the process of reformatting the company's various drives when the intrusion was discovered and the servers disconnected from the internet.

Critical vendor partners should be monitored for new business relationships, financial results, organizational changes and governmental associations. All external supplier companies and consultant firms should be monitored and include content analysis of social media (e.g., *LinkedIn, Facebook, Twitter,* and *Youtube*) using tools such as *Maltego* and **content scraping** and search engines like *Devon Technologies*.

7. Monitor the Process Equipment Looking for Anomalies

It is probably easier to detect a cyber-physical attack (when it occurs) by looking at how the equipment is operating than it is to detect subtle software anomalies or dropped packets. Although boiler water temperature and pressure rising dangerous levels doesn't necessarily signal that a cyber-physical attack is underway, it could be an attack. Don't assume it isn't a cyber-attack out of hand. Look for signs that the controls have been manipulated. Compare what the computer *says* is happening with what the equipment is actually doing. Remember, a sneaky attacker will change the *setpoints* higher than normal so the computer will not *know* something is wrong.

Malicious attackers are more likely to use the process control systems to make equipment "*misbehave*" while appearing to operate normally. At the Iranian nuclear plant, *Stuxnet* manipulated the *calibration systems* so the plant workers didn't see the real pressure readings that would have flagged the problems with the devices early on. Had the workers manually checked the equipment itself frequently, they would have noticed the discrepancy.

A malicious attacker would schedule his attack when it would be *less likely to be detected* or when it could *do the most damage*. *Startup and shutdown* of a process plant are the two most dangerous operational modes of the plant. A well-qualified attacker would know the planned startup sequence of operations and manipulate the amount of heat or the flow of chemicals to corrupt *the process* and damage *the hardware*.

For example, industrial distillation is typically performed in large, vertical cylindrical columns known as *distillation towers* or *distillation columns*. The amount of heat entering a distillation column is a crucial operating parameter, addition of *excess or insufficient heat* to the column can lead to *foaming, weeping, entrainment, or flooding*. If the column contains liquid during *pressuring*, excessive vapor flows will cause *flooding* and *gas lifting of the liquid*, resulting in liquid discharge into *relief header* and damage the column internals.

8. What to do When the Shit Hits the Fan Coil Unit

Accept the fact that eventually your facility will be the target of a cyber-physical attack. The only choices you have in this matter are *how* your building will be attacked (by reducing the number of possible *attack vectors*), how you will *respond* to an attack, and how you will *recover* from an attack.

When a cyber-physical attack occurs, the last thing you want to do is make things up as you go. The time to figure out what must be done when an attack happens is not during a crisis. Decide NOW the actions that need to be taken when you first detect a cyber-physical attack so you can make decisions quickly and take proper action to mitigate the impact of the attack. Prepare a written, customized **Recovery Procedures Plan** that includes detailed responsibilities and specific tasks for emergency response activities and building resumption operations based upon pre-defined time frames. Your employees should know how to react when a building is attacked.

For more detailed information on Recovery Procedures Plans and a template to prepare your own custom plan, see my other book titled, *"Cyber-Physical Attack Recovery Procedures."*

For strategies for **forensic evidence of a cyber-physical attack**, see my other book titled, *"Cybersecurity for Hospitals and Healthcare Facilities."*

Key Takeaways

1. Patching a server could disrupt the BCS software so they are often unpatched resulting in vulnerabilities remaining that would normally be patched. Install software **patches** as soon as they are released and keep a log.
2. Make frequent **backups** of important files.
3. BCS's are often installed without the IT department's knowledge.
4. IT staff is unfamiliar with BCS's and they don't know if the connection to a port is normal, so it is often ignored.
5. The only reason a BCS should be connected to the Internet is when you are *trying* to be hacked and you *want* to experience a cyber-physical attack.
6. Be ready to go completely off the grid at a moments notice.

ATTACK VECTORS & BCS RELATED JARGON

Note: A more complete list of cybersecurity jargon is available in my other book: *"Cybersecurity Lexicon"*, published by APRESS.

Account Sitting - The practice of letting someone log in to your account if you're going to be away. Since they have nearly full access to your account there is a potential for them to do a lot of damage.

Active Medical Devices (AMD) - An active medical device is one that interfaces directly with a patient to administer medical treatment. Examples of AMDs are: X-Ray machine, MRI, CT Scanner, Pet Scanner, infusion pumps, surgical lasers, medical ventilators, extracorporeal membrane oxygenation machines and dialysis machines. Many active medical devices today include a computer to control the machine and communicate with the hospital network, so it is possible for them to be hacked. See my book *"Cybersecurity for Hospitals and Healthcare Facilities"* for more information.

Active Patient Monitoring Devices - These are networked in-hospital patient monitoring devices that require a timely response (e.g. a monitor that is intended to detect life-threatening arrhythmias such as ventricular fibrillation or a device used to actively monitor diabetes for time-sensitive intervention). These devices can be hacked. See my book *"Cybersecurity for Hospitals and Healthcare Facilities"* for more information.

Adversarial Images - Used in the field of computer vision, researchers from Google, Facebook, and academia found that if they first presented an AI computer-brain with an image it could recognize and then modified the pixels ever so slightly, the algorithm could be tricked into misclassifying the second image, even though if placed side by side, the images would look identical to the human eye. That means that, statistically, next to every classifiable image is a virtually indistinguishable one that a neural network can't recognize. According to Alexey Kurakin, one of the authors of the report and researcher at *Google Brain*, "Let's say an image of an elephant," he continued. "You modify the image slightly with this noise that is hard for the human eye to see very well. [If] you give it to your image recognition system, now the image recognition system thinks it's no longer an elephant, but an airplane or a car," even though a human eye likely wouldn't be confused by the same trick. The human mind is extremely difficult to reverse engineer, and we're not anywhere close to fully modeling its intricacies.

Researchers have engineered a similar way to fool AI trained to understand human language. A team of computer scientists in Beijing found a way to fool a computer trained to understand language. By adding one very specific word to a particular part of a long sentence, or slightly misspelling one word in a phrase (such as change "film" to "flim"), a computer trained to say whether a sentence is about buildings or corporations will completely flip its analysis. SOURCE: Motherboard

AFK (away from keyboard) - *Hackerspeak* used in chat situations to notify others that you will be momentarily unavailable online.

Alarm Notifications - BCS alarms tend to fall into one of four categories:
    True Positive – Something bad happened and the IDS caught it.
    True Negative – The event is benign and no alert was generated.
    False Positive – The IDS alert sounded, but the event was not malicious.
    False Negative - Something bad happened, the IDS didn't catch it.

"All your base are belong to us." - *Hackerspeak* for a declaration of victory or superiority. The origin is from what many consider to be the worst Japanese-to-English translation in video game history - "Zero Wing" arcade game for the Sega Genesis. SOURCE: The Jargon File (version 4.4.7)

Android Things (codenamed Brillo) - This is an *Android*-based embedded operating system platform by *Google*. It is aimed to be used with low-power and memory constrained *Internet of Things (IoT)* devices. *Brillo* takes the usual Android development stack—*Android Studio*, the official *SDK*, and *Google Play Services*—and applies it to the IoT. As an IoT *OS* it is designed to work as low as 32-64 MB of RAM. It will support *Bluetooth low energy* and *Wi-Fi*. *Android Things* allows developers to build a *smart device* using *Android APIs* and *Google Services*. Every Android device will automatically recognize any *Brillo OS device*, so user can easily choose a device, set it up and use it immediately.

ASCII Armoring - Binary-to-text encoding of messages that are already plain text, then decoding on the other end, one can make such systems appear to be completely transparent. This is sometimes referred to as ASCII armoring. Binary-to-text encoding is encoding of data in plain text. More precisely, it is an encoding of binary data in a sequence of printable characters.

Attractive Nuisance Doctrine - Applies to the law of torts, in the United States. It states that a landowner may be held liable for injuries to children trespassing on the land if the injury is caused by an object on the land that is likely to attract children. Although this has not been applied to cyberspace as of yet, a smart attorney eventually will attempt to use this as a hacking defense. If the argument holds up in court, for example, a hospital may be found legally liable if their network has little or no cybersecurity defense and is an attractive target which lured script kiddies onto the hospital's network. In lay terms: the hospital knows or has reason to know children are around that might hack into the network; the hospital knows the network is not secure; the children are too young to know the danger (to patients); the problem can be avoided at reasonable cost; and the hospital fails to exercise reasonable caution. Although there have been instances in the media of hospitals being hacked, the "open and obvious" rule may not be an exception because patients are unaware of the possible danger and the hospital has a "duty to warn" patients. This example is purely hypothetical as this would be unsettled legal theory, not "black letter law."

Authority Having Jurisdiction (AHJ) - Authority Having Jurisdiction is defined as "An organization, office, or individual responsible for enforcing the requirements of a code or standard, or for approving equipment, materials, an installation, or a procedure." The AHJ is not a single entity. Depending on the jurisdiction your facility is in, the type of facility you're in, and who "owns" your facility, you may be visited not only by the fire marshal, but by a variety of individuals — referred to as "the authority having jurisdiction" — who come onto the premises to look at how well or how poorly your fire, life, and electrical safety programs are doing. SOURCE: National Electrical Code & National Fire Protection Association

Automatic Sequential Control System - Triggers a series of mechanical actuators in the proper sequence to perform a task. For example, various electric and pneumatic transducers may fold and glue a cardboard box, fill it with product and then seal it in an automatic packaging machine.

Automagically - *Hackerspeak* for automatically, but in a way that, for some reason (typically because it is too complicated, or too ugly, or perhaps too trivial), the speaker doesn't feel like explaining to you. SOURCE: The Jargon File (version 4.4.7)

Automated Security Monitoring - Use of automated procedures to ensure security controls are not circumvented or the use of these tools to track actions taken by subjects suspected of misusing the information system.

Automatic Remote Rekeying - Procedure to rekey distant cryptographic equipment electronically without specific actions by the receiving terminal operator.

Bad and Wrong - *Hackerspeak* for something that is both badly designed and wrongly executed. This common term is the prototype of, and is used by contrast with, three less common terms — *Bad and Right* (a kludge, something ugly but functional); *Good and Wrong* (an overblown GUI or other attractive nuisance); and (rare praise) *Good and Right*. SOURCE: The Jargon File (version 4.4.7)

banana problem - *Hackerspeak* for not knowing where or when to bring a production to a close. One may say there is a banana problem of an algorithm with poorly defined or incorrect termination conditions, or in discussing the evolution of a design that may be succumbing to "featuritis". From the story of the little girl who said "I know how to spell 'banana', but I don't know when to stop." SOURCE: The Jargon File (version 4.4.7)

barfmail - *Hackerspeak* for multiple bounce messages accumulating to the level of serious annoyance, or worse. SOURCE: The Jargon File (version 4.4.7)

Bash Bunny - A *USB drive* that emulates combinations of trusted USB devices — like *gigabit Ethernet*, *serial, flash storage* and *keyboards* so computers are tricked into divulging data, exfiltrating documents, installing backdoors and many more *exploits*. Slide the switch to your payload of choice, plug the *Bash Bunny* into the victim computer and watch the multi-color LED. With a quad-core CPU and desktop-class SSD it goes from *plug to pwn* in 7 seconds.

Bastard Operator From Hell (BOFH) - *Hackerspeak* refers to a system administrator with absolutely no tolerance for *lusers*. SOURCE: The Jargon File (version 4.4.7)

Batbelt - Many hackers routinely hang numerous devices such as pagers, cell-phones, personal organizers, Leatherman multitools, pocket knives, flashlights, walkie-talkies, even miniature computers from their belts. When many of these devices are worn at once, the hacker's belt somewhat resembles Batman's utility belt. SOURCE: The Jargon File (version 4.4.7)

Beacon - A beacon is similar to a *geo-fence*, but on a micro level. These devices, consume little power and the underlying communication technology is *Bluetooth Low Energy*. The signal transmitted by these devices can be detected by smartphones and utilized to trigger actions within apps. In essence, beacon technology allows Mobile Apps to understand their position on a micro-local scale, and deliver hyper-contextual content to a *location-aware device* based on location. Due to the open nature of the signal broadcasting from a beacon, spoofing or cloning beacon identifiers is fairly easy.

Benign Environment - A non-hostile location protected from external hostile elements by physical, personnel, and procedural security countermeasures.

Berzerkeley - *Hackerspeak*, a humorous distortion of "Berkeley" used esp. to refer to the practices or products of the BSD Unix hackers. SOURCE: The Jargon File (version 4.4.7)

Bikeshedding - *Hackerspeak* referring to technical disputes over minor, marginal issues conducted while more serious ones are being overlooked. The implied image is of people arguing over what color to paint the bicycle shed while the house is not finished. SOURCE: The Jargon File (version 4.4.7)

Bitcoin - Bitcoin is a *cryptocurrency* and an electronic payment system. The system is *peer-to-peer*, and transactions take place between users directly, without an intermediary. These transactions are verified by network nodes and recorded in a public distributed ledger called the *blockchain*, which uses bitcoin as its unit of account. Since the system works without a central repository or single administrator, bitcoin is called the first *decentralized digital currency*. The use of bitcoin by criminals has been well documented.

Black Magic - *Hackerspeak* refers to a technique that works, though nobody really understands why. More obscure than *voodoo programming*, which may be done by cookbook. SOURCE: The Jargon File (version 4.4.7)

Bloatware - *Hackerspeak* for software that provides minimal functionality while requiring a disproportionate amount of diskspace and memory. Especially used for application and OS upgrades. SOURCE: The Jargon File (version 4.4.7)

Blockchain - A *blockchain* is a *decentralized digital ledger* for *cryptocurrency* that records transactions across many computers (*nodes*) in such a way that the registered transactions cannot be altered retroactively. Network *nodes* can validate transactions, add them to their copy of the ledger, and then broadcast *blocks* of these ledger additions to other *nodes* approximately six times per hour. *Blockchains* have been described as a *value-exchange protocol*. This exchange of value can be completed more quickly, more safely and more cheaply with a *blockchain*.

Blog - A truncation of the expression "*weblog*". A blog is a discussion or informational website published on the World Wide Web consisting of discrete, often informal diary-style text entries ("*posts*"). Posts are typically displayed in reverse chronological order, so that the most recent post appears first, at the top of the web page.

Blowout Panels - These are areas with intentionally weakened structure, are used in enclosures, buildings or vehicles where a sudden overpressure may occur. By failing in a predictable manner, they channel the overpressure or pressure wave in the direction where it causes controlled, directed minimal harm, instead of causing a catastrophic failure of the structure. Also, called *blow-off panels*.

Blue Box - A blue box is a tool that emerged in the 1960s and '70s; it allowed users to route their own calls to place free telephone calls. A related device, the black box enabled one to receive calls which were free to the caller. The blue box no longer works as modern switching systems are now digital and do not use in-band signaling.

Bluetooth Low Energy - This is a wireless *personal area network* technology used for transmitting data over short distances. As the name implies, it's designed for low energy consumption and cost, while maintaining a communication range similar to that of its predecessor, Classic *Bluetooth*.

bottom-up implementation - *Hackerspeak* for the opposite of a top-down design. *Hackers* often find that it works best to build things in the opposite order, by writing and testing a clean set of primitive operations and then knitting them together. Naively applied, this leads to hacked-together *bottom-up* implementations; a more sophisticated response is *middle-out* implementation, in which scratch code within primitives at the mid-level of the system is gradually replaced with a more polished version of the lowest level at the same time the structure above the midlevel is being built. SOURCE: The Jargon File (version 4.4.7)

bread crumbs - Debugging statements inserted into a program that emit output or log indicators of the program's state to a file so you can see where it dies or pin down the cause of surprising behavior.

breath-of-life packet - *Hackerspeak* for an *Ethernet* packet that contains boot code, periodically sent out from a working computer to infuse the 'breath of life' into any computer on the network that has happened to crash. Machines depending on such packets have sufficient hardware or firmware code to wait for (or request) such a packet during the reboot process. The opposite is the *kiss-of-death packet* used for dealing with hosts that consume too many network resources. SOURCE: The Jargon File (version 4.4.7)

Broadcast Storm - *Hackerspeak* refers to when an incorrect packet broadcast on a network causes most hosts to respond all at once, typically with wrong answers that start the process over again.

Browser Helper Objects (BHO) - This is a *DLL* module designed as a plugin for *Microsoft's Internet Explorer* web browser to provide added functionality. The *Adobe Acrobat* plug-in that allows *Internet Explorer* users to read PDF files within their browser is a BHO. Commonly used by threats to spy on or interfere with web browsing.

Brute Force and Ignorance - *Hackerspeak* for a popular design technique at many software houses — brute force coding unrelieved by any knowledge of how problems have been previously solved in elegant ways. SOURCE: The Jargon File (version 4.4.7)

Bug Compatible - *Hackerspeak* for a design or revision that has been badly compromised by a requirement to be compatible with *fossils* or *misfeatures* in other programs or (esp.) previous releases of itself. SOURCE: The Jargon File (version 4.4.7)

Burble - *Hackerspeak* connotes that the source is truly clueless and ineffectual (mere *flamers* can be competent). A term of deep contempt. SOURCE: The Jargon File (version 4.4.7)

Buried Treasure - *Hackerspeak* for a surprising piece of code found in some program. Used sarcastically, because what is found is anything but treasure. While usually not wrong, it tends to minor to major errors, and has lain undiscovered only because it was functionally correct, however horrible it is. Buried treasure almost always needs to be dug up and removed. SOURCE: The Jargon File (version 4.4.7)

Bus - The main electrical communication path in which signals are sent from one part of the computer to another. Field-level buses can be grouped in three categories, depending on the device type and application for which they were designed:
- **Sensor Bus** - Sensor buses are common in discrete manufacturing. They're used with proximity switches,
pushbuttons, motor starters, and other simple devices where costs must be minimized and only a few bits of information need to be transmitted. These buses usually cover short to medium distances, using either 2 or 4 wires. They typically are not intrinsically safe.
- **Device Bus** - Device buses are designed to meet the needs of more-complex devices, often in fast-moving discrete operations requiring short, fast communications. Paper machines, packaging lines, and motor control centers often use this type of bus. Device buses are usually 4-wire and not intrinsically safe. They can communicate at high speed for short distances, and slower speeds for longer distances.
- **Fieldbus** - Most appropriate for control and diagnostics in process operations. Fieldbuses provide highly reliable two-way communications between "smart" devices and systems in time-critical applications. They're optimized for messages containing several floating-point variables — all sampled at the same time — and the status of each variable.

Business Impact Analysis (BIA) - The process of analyzing all business functions and the effect that a specific disaster or cyber-attack may have upon them.

Business Interruption - Any event, whether anticipated (i.e., public service strike) or unanticipated (i.e., blackout) which disrupts the normal course of business operations at a corporate location.

Business Interruption Costs - The costs or lost revenue associated with an interruption in normal business operations.

Business Recovery Process - The common critical path that all companies follow during a recovery effort. There are major nodes along the path that are followed regardless of the organization. The process has seven stages: 1) Immediate response, 2) Environmental restoration, 3) Functional restoration, 4) Data synchronization, 5) Restore business functions, 6) Interim site, and 7) Return home.

Business Recovery Team - A group of individuals responsible for maintaining and coordinating the recovery process. Similar Terms: Recovery Team

Business Resumption Planning (BRP) - The operations piece of business continuity planning. Also see: *Disaster Recovery Planning*

Business Unit Recovery - The component of disaster recovery which deals specifically with the relocation of key organization personnel in the event of a disaster, and the provision of essential records, equipment supplies, work space, communication facilities, computer processing capability, etc. Similar Terms: Work Group Recovery.

Cable Monkey - Derogatory *Hackerspeak* meaning an installer's employee that pulls cable thru a building for networking or telco purposes.

Cable Tray - See *Wire Ladder*.

Can't happen - *Hackerspeak* refers to the traditional programmer comment for code executed under a condition that should never be true, for example a file size computed as negative. Often, such a condition being true indicates data corruption or a faulty algorithm; it is almost always handled by emitting a fatal error message and terminating or crashing, since there is little else that can be done. Some case variant of "can't happen" is also often the text emitted if the 'impossible' error actually happens! SOURCE: The Jargon File (version 4.4.7)

Captive Portal - A web page which is displayed to newly connected users before they are granted broader access to network resources such as at a hotel. Captive portals have been known to have incomplete firewall rule sets. An attempt to authenticate with incorrect or obsolete credentials usually results in account locking. A good place to have credentials stolen.

Careware - *Hackerspeak* for a variety of shareware for which either the author suggests that some payment be made to a nominated charity or a levy directed to charity is included on top of the distribution charge. SOURCE: The Jargon File (version 4.4.7)

Cascade Control Loop - In a *single-loop control*, the controller's *setpoint* is set by an operator, and its output drives a final control element. For example, a *level controller* driving a *control valve* to keep the level at its *setpoint*. In a *cascade control* arrangement, there are two (or more) controllers of which one controller's *output* drives the *setpoint* of another controller. For example: a level controller driving the *setpoint* of a flow controller to keep the level at its *setpoint*. The flow controller, in turn, drives a control valve to match the flow with the *setpoint* the level controller is requesting. The controller *driving the setpoint* (the level controller) is called the *primary, outer*, or *master controller*. The controller *receiving the setpoint* (flow controller) is called the *secondary, inner* or *slave* controller. A *cascade control loop* is used when a process with relatively slow dynamics (like level, temperature, composition, humidity) and a liquid or gas flow, or some other relatively-fast process, has to be manipulated to control the slow process.

Casters-Up Mode - *Hackerspeak* for 'broken' or 'down'. Usually connotes a major failure. A system (hardware or software) which is down may be already being restarted before the failure is noticed, whereas one which is casters- up is usually a good excuse to take the rest of the day off. SOURCE: The Jargon File (version 4.4.7)

Censys - *Censys* is a *search engine* designed to search for Internet-connected devices. It collects data using both *ZMap* and *ZGrab* (an application layer scanner that operates via *ZMap*), which in this case scan the *IPV4* address space. *Censys* can perform full-text searches. Here are two sample searches: https://www.censys.io/ipv4?q=80.http.get.status_code%3A%20200 – this allows you to search for all hosts with a specific HTTP status code. You can also just type in an IP address, such as: "66.24.206.155" or "71.20.34.200" (those are fake). To find hosts in 23.0.0.0/8 and 8.8.8.0/24, type in "23.0.0.0/8 or 8.8.8.0/24."

Certification and Accreditation (C&A) - Certification and Accreditation is a federally mandated standard process designed to ensure that national security information systems meet documented security requirements and maintain the accredited security posture throughout their system life cycle. Since *C&A* is mandated upon all systems of the federal government, often it is taken as just a required step in order to stand up an information technology system, and no longer considered once the process is complete. However, *C&A*, if taken in its intended spirit, can be an invaluable tool to manage the security of a system throughout its life cycle. Much of the process of a formal *C&A* could easily be applied to the commercial world

to better understand and manage the security posture of any publicly exposed information technology system.
- **Certification** - The technical evaluation of the security components and their compliance for Accreditation.
- **Accreditation** - The formal acceptance of the adequacy of the system's overall security by management.

Chain of Trust - This is established by validating each component of hardware and software from the bottom up. It is intended to ensure that only trusted software and hardware can be used while still retaining flexibility. It starts with hardware that will only boot from software that is digitally signed.

Chemical Feed Pump Hack - A chemical feed pump is a relay- or *proportionally-controlled pump* that disperses chemical into the system. A cracker can slow or stop the flow, or he can speed it up. Any change in the correct flow will result in process failure and lost product.

Chernobyl Packet - *Hackerspeak* for a network packet that induces a broadcast storm and/or network meltdown, in memory of the April 1986 nuclear accident at Chernobyl in Ukraine. The typical scenario involves an *IP Ethernet datagram* that passes through a *gateway* with both source and destination *Ether* and *IP address* set as the respective broadcast addresses for the *subnetworks* being gated between. SOURCE: The Jargon File (version 4.4.7)

Cipher - Any cryptographic system in which arbitrary symbols or groups of symbols, represent units of plain text, or in which units of plain text are rearranged, or both. SOURCE: CNSSI No. 4009

Closed Security Environment - Environment providing sufficient assurance that applications and equipment are protected against the introduction of malicious logic during an information system life cycle. Closed security is based upon a system's developers, operators, and maintenance personnel having sufficient clearances, authorization, and configuration control. SOURCE: CNSSI No. 4009

Cloudbleed - A security flaw that exposed the private information of millions of Internet users worldwide. *Cloudbleed* leaked information like passwords, message contents, and more before it was discovered.

Code - *Hackerspeak* for the stuff that software writers write, either in source form or after translation by a compiler or assembler. Often used in opposition to "data", which is the stuff that code operates on. Among hackers this is a mass noun, as in "How much code does it take to do a bubble sort?" Among scientific programmers it is sometimes a count noun equivalent to "program"; thus they may speak of "codes" in the plural. Anyone referring to software as "the software codes" is probably a *newbie* or a *suit*. To write code. In this sense, always refers to source code rather than compiled. SOURCE: The Jargon File (version 4.4.7)

Code Injection - The exploitation of a computer bug that is caused by processing invalid data. Injection is used by an attacker to introduce (or "inject") code into a vulnerable computer program and change the course of execution. The result of successful code injection is often disastrous (for instance: code injection is used by some computer worms to propagate). Code injection vulnerabilities (*injection flaws*) occur when an application sends untrusted data to an interpreter. Injection flaws are most often found in SQL, LDAP, XPath, or NoSQL queries; OS commands; XML parsers, SMTP headers, program arguments, etc. Injection flaws tend to be easier to discover when examining source code than via testing. *Scanners* and *fuzzers* can help attackers find injection flaws. Injection can result in data loss or corruption, lack of accountability, denial of access and can sometimes lead to complete host takeover.

Code Monkey - *Hackerspeak* for a person only capable of grinding out code, but unable to perform the higher-primate tasks of software architecture, analysis, and design. Mildly insulting. A programmer. SOURCE: The Jargon File (version 4.4.7)

Collaborative Automation System (CAS) - See *CPAS*.

Collaborative Process Automation System (CPAS) - CPAS offer a single, unified environment for the presentation of information to the operator as well as the ability to present information in context "to the right people at the right time" from any point within the system. *Distributed Control Systems (DCSs)* evolved into *Process Automation Systems (PAS)* by the inclusion of additional functionality beyond basic control. The evolution of *PAS* into *CPAS* is thought to add more capability. *CPAS* is expected to become the primary source of manufacturing data and information for *Collaborative Manufacturing Management (CMM)* applications.

Collaborative Manufacturing Management (CMM) - *CMM* is the practice of managing by controlling the key business and manufacturing processes of a manufacturing enterprise in the context of its value networks. *CMM* is focused on facilitating and *managing business processes first*, and the *supporting systems second.* CMM is said to improve response to changing market conditions, streamline product introductions, improve asset utilization, increase or maintain market share, reduce inventory and reduce cycle times.

Co-Lo - Short for 'co-location', used of a machine you own that is physically sited on the premises of an *ISP* in order to take advantage of the ISP's direct access to lots of network bandwidth. Often in the phrases co-lo box or co-lo machines. *Co-lo boxes* are typically web and *FTP servers* remote-administered by their owners, who may seldom or never visit the actual site.

Common Cause Failure (CCF) - CCF is a slow process caused by corrosion or premature wear of mechanical components. A second-order CCF such as motors and pumps that to cease to function when commercial power is lost. CCF does not apply to software because software does not wear out.

Common Criteria for Information Technology Security Evaluation (CC) - An international standard (ISO/IEC 15408) for computer security certification. Common Criteria is a framework in which computer system users can specify their *security functional* and *assurance requirements (SFRs and SARs* respectively) through the use of *Protection Profiles (PPs)*, vendors can then implement and/or make claims about the security attributes of their products, and testing laboratories can evaluate the products to determine if they actually meet the claims. In other words, Common Criteria provides assurance that the process of specification, implementation and evaluation of a computer security product has been conducted in a rigorous and standard and repeatable manner at a level that is commensurate with the target environment for use. Common Criteria is used as the basis for a Government-driven certification scheme and typically evaluations are conducted for the use of Federal Government agencies and critical infrastructure.

Compensating Security Control - A management, operational, and/or technical control (i.e., safeguard or countermeasure) employed by an organization in lieu of a recommended security control in the low, moderate, or high baselines described in NIST Special Publication 800-53 or in CNSS Instruction 1253, that provides equivalent or comparable protection for an information system. SOURCE: NIST SP 800.53

Computer Security (COMPUSEC) - Measures and controls that ensure confidentiality, integrity, and availability of information system assets including hardware, software, firmware, and information being processed, stored, and communicated. SOURCE: CNSSI No. 4009

Computer Vision - *Artificial Intelligence (AI)* focused on image processing. The goal is to achieve human-level understanding of an image. *Google* researchers found that the accuracy of the company's image recognition algorithms often failed when they were challenged with grainy, less-than-perfect pictures and previous research has shown that a computer can be made to think a stop sign is a yield sign.

Concise Binary Object Representation (CBOR) - CBOR is a data format whose design goals include the possibility of extremely small code size, fairly small message size, and extensibility without the need for version negotiation. CBOR is based on the *JSON* data model: numbers, strings, arrays, maps (called objects in *JSON*), and a few values such as false, true, and null. CBOR itself is encoded in binary to reduce size and allow faster processing.

Confinement Channel - An unauthorized communication path that manipulates a communications medium in an unexpected, unconventional or unforeseen way in order to transmit information without detection by anyone other than the entities operating the covert channel. SOURCE: CNSSI No. 4009

Connected Car Hack - Automakers and third-party developers have released *Android apps* that turn *smartphones* into vehicular remote controls, allowing drivers to locate, lock, and unlock their rides with a screen tap. Unfortunately, *smartphones* can be hacked and most of those apps lack even basic software defenses. The apps typically store the unencrypted user name and password on the smartphone. By tricking a user into installing malicious code or by *rooting* the target phone, *crackers* could use the app to locate a car, unlock it, and in some cases, start its ignition. Also, see *Passive Keyless Entry* and *overlay attack*. SOURCE: Kaspersky

Connected Lighting Systems - See *ZigBee Light Link*.

Constrained Application Protocol (CoAP) - The CoAP is a specialized web transfer protocol for use with constrained nodes and constrained networks in the Internet of Things. The protocol is designed for machine-to-machine (M2M) applications such as smart energy and building automation. CoAP has been designed to work on microcontrollers with as low as 10 KiB of RAM and 100 KiB of code space. Servers make resources available under a URL, and clients access these resources using methods such as GET, PUT, POST, and DELETE. CoAP feels very much like HTTP. Obtaining a value from a sensor is not much different from obtaining a value from a web API. CoAP is designed to use minimal resources, both on the device and on the network. Instead of a complex transport stack, it gets by with UDP on IP. A 4-byte fixed header and a compact encoding of options enables small messages that cause no or little fragmentation on the link layer. Many servers can operate in a completely stateless fashion. CoAP provides strong security using DTLS parameters equivalent to 3072-bit RSA keys.

Container - Used by software developers, everything required to make a piece of software run is packaged into isolated *containers*. *Containers* do not bundle a full operating system - only libraries and settings required to make the software work. This guarantees that software will always run the same, regardless of where it's deployed. A good example is *Docker*.

Control Flow Guard (CFG) - CFG is a highly-optimized platform security feature in Windows that was created to combat memory corruption vulnerabilities. By placing tight restrictions on where an application can execute code from, it makes it much harder for exploits to execute arbitrary code through vulnerabilities such as buffer overflows. CFG extends previous exploit mitigation technologies such as /GS, DEP, and ASLR. Runs on "CFG-Aware" versions of Windows. When a CFG check fails at runtime, *Windows* immediately terminates the program, thus breaking any exploit that attempts to indirectly call an invalid address.

Control Loop - A *control loop* is a process management system designed to maintain a process variable at a desired *setpoint*. Each step in the loop works in conjunction with the others to manage the system.

Control System - A control system that manages, commands, directs or regulates the behavior of other devices or systems for controlling processes or machines. In an *open loop control system*, the control action from the controller is independent of the "process output". For example, a boiler controlled only by a timer. In a *closed loop control system*, the control action from the controller is dependent on the desired and actual process output values, such as when the building temperature is set on the thermostat. The desired temperature programmed into the thermostat is called the *setpoint* or *reference input*. *Closed loop controllers* are also called *feedback controllers*.

Control Valve - A control valve is a valve used to control fluid flow by varying the size of the flow passage as directed by a signal from a controller. This enables the direct control of flow rate and the consequential control of process quantities such as pressure, temperature, and liquid level. In automatic control terminology, a control valve is termed a *"final control element"*. Taking as an example an air-operated valve, there are two *control actions* possible:

Air or current to open - The flow restriction decreases with increased control signal value.

Air or current to close - The flow restriction increases with increased control signal value.

There can also be failure to *safety modes*:

Failure to open - On failure of compressed air to actuator, valve opens under spring pressure or backup power.

Failure to close - On failure of compressed air to actuator, valve closes under spring pressure or backup power.

Controller Area Network (CANBUS) - A vehicle bus standard designed to allow microcontrollers and devices to communicate with each other in applications without a host computer. It is a message-based protocol, designed originally for multiplex electrical wiring within automobiles, but is also used in many other contexts. The modern automobile may have as many as 70 electronic control units (ECU) for various subsystems. Typically, the biggest processor is the engine control unit.

Cookie Jar - An area of memory set aside for storing *cookies*.

Cooling Tower - A cooling tower is a heat rejection device which rejects waste heat to the atmosphere through the cooling of a water stream to a lower temperature. Cooling towers use the evaporation of water to remove process heat and cool the working fluid to near the wet-bulb air temperature or, in the case of closed circuit dry cooling towers, rely solely on air to cool the working fluid to near the dry-bulb air temperature.

Continuous Diagnostics and Mitigation (CDM) - The CDM program is a dynamic approach to fortifying the cybersecurity of networks and systems. CDM provides users with capabilities and tools that identify cybersecurity risks on an ongoing basis, prioritize these risks based upon potential impacts, and enable cybersecurity personnel to mitigate the most significant problems first. Network *sensors* perform an automated search for known cyber flaws. Results feed into a local dashboard that produces customized reports, alerting network managers to their worst and most critical cyber risks based on standardized and weighted risk scores.

Prioritized alerts enable agencies to efficiently allocate resources based on the severity of the risk. Progress reports track results, which can be used to compare security posture among department networks. Summary information can feed into an enterprise-level dashboard to inform and situational awareness into cybersecurity risk posture across the company. SOURCE: DHS

Control Network - The *control network* hosts all the devices that on one side control the actuators and sensors of the physical layer and on the other side provide the control interface to the *process network*. The *process network* usually hosts the *SCADA* servers and human-machine interfaces.

Covert Storage Channel - *Covert channel* involving the direct or indirect writing to a storage location by one process and the direct or indirect reading of the storage location by another process. *Covert storage channels* typically involve a finite resource (e.g., sectors on a disk) that is shared by two subjects at different security levels. SOURCE: CNSSI-4009

Cowboy - Synonym for *hacker*. It is reported that at *Sun* this word is often said with reverence. SOURCE: The Jargon File (version 4.4.7)

Cracker - A *hacker* that breaks into computers for criminal gain. Also, someone who breaks into someone else's computer system, bypasses passwords or licenses in computer programs; or in other ways intentionally breaches computer security. *Cracker* also refers to those that reverse engineer software and modify it for grins and giggles.

Cracker Slang - Often called "*leet-speak*", so the reader will be able to understand both what leaks out of the *cracker* underground and the occasional ironic use by *hackers*. Here is a brief guide to *cracker* usage:

- Misspell frequently. The substitutions phone → fone and freak → phreak are obligatory.
- Always substitute 'z' s for 's' s. (i.e. "codes" → "codez"). The substitution of 'z' for 's' has evolved so that a 'z' is now systematically put at the end of words to denote an illegal or cracking connection. Examples: Appz, passwordz, passez, utilz, MP3z, distroz, pornz, sitez, gamez, crackz, serialz, downloadz, FTPz, etc.
- Type random emphasis characters after a post line (i.e. "Hey Dudes!#!$#$!#!$").
- Use the emphatic 'k' prefix ("k-kool", "k-rad", "k-awesome") frequently.

- Abbreviate compulsively ("I got lotsa warez w/ docs").

The following letter substitutions are common:

a → 4
e → 3
f → ph
i → 1 or |
l → | or 1
m → |V|
n → |\|
o → 0
  s → 5
t → 7 or +

Thus, "elite" comes out "31337" and *all your base are belong to us*
becomes "4ll y0ur b4s3 4r3 b3l0ng t0 us",
Other less common substitutions include:

b → 8
c → (or k or |< or /<
d → <|
g → 6 or 9
h → |-|
k → |< or /<
p → |2
u → |_|
v → / or V
w → // or W
x → ><
y → '/

SOURCE: The Jargon File (version 4.4.7)

Cracking - Illegally breaking into a computer system. Contrary to widespread myth, this does not usually involve some mysterious leap of *hackerly* brilliance, but rather persistence and the dogged repetition of a handful of fairly well-known tricks that exploit common weaknesses in the security of target systems. Accordingly, most *crackers* are said to be incompetent as *hackers*. SOURCE: The Jargon File (version 4.4.7)

Crack Root - *Hackerspeak* to defeat the security system of a Unix machine and gain root privileges. SOURCE: The Jargon File (version 4.4.7)

Crap Flooding - Posting nonsensical or repetitive postings online making it difficult for legitimate users to read other postings and suppressing relevant content.

Crapplet - *Hackerspeak* describing a worthless applet, esp. a Java widget attached to a web page that doesn't work or even crashes your browser. Also, spelled 'craplet'. SOURCE: The Jargon File (version 4.4.7)

Crawling Horror - *Hackerspeak* describing ancient hardware or software that is kept obstinately alive by forces beyond the control of the hackers at a site. SOURCE: The Jargon File (version 4.4.7)

Crippleware - *Hackerspeak* describing software that has some important functionality deliberately removed, so as to entice potential users to pay for a working version. SOURCE: The Jargon File (version 4.4.7)

Crossload - *Hackerspeak* for moving files between machines on a peer-to-peer network of nodes that act as both servers and clients for a distributed file store. SOURCE: The Jargon File (version 4.4.7)

Cryppie - *Hackerspeak* for a cryptographer. One who hacks or implements cryptographic software or hardware. SOURCE: The Jargon File (version 4.4.7)

Cup Holder - *Hackerspeak* for the tray of a CD-ROM drive, or by extension the CD drive itself. So, called because of a common tech support legend about the idiot who called to complain that the cup holder on his computer broke. SOURCE: The Jargon File (version 4.4.7)

CV Dazzle - CV Dazzle explores how fashion can be used as camouflage from *automated face-detection* technology via expressive interference that combines highly stylized makeup and hair styling with face-detection thwarting designs. CV Dazzle uses avant-garde hairstyling and makeup designs to break apart the continuity of a face. Since *facial-recognition algorithms* rely on the identification and spatial relationship of key facial features, like symmetry and tonal contours, one can block detection by creating an *"anti-face"*. In the animal kingdom, this inverse effect is known as *countershading*. Here are some key techniques to decrease your probability of being detected:

- **Avoid enhancers** - They amplify key facial features. This makes your face easier to detect. Instead apply makeup that contrasts with your skin tone in unusual tones and directions: light colors on dark skin, dark colors on light skin.
- **Partially obscure the nose-bridge area** - The region where the nose, eyes, and forehead intersect is a key facial feature.
- **Partially obscure one of the ocular regions** - The position and darkness of eyes is a key facial feature.
- **Modify the contrast of your face** - Tonal gradients, and spatial relationship of dark and light areas using hair, makeup, and/or unique fashion accessories.
- **Obscure the elliptical shape of a head** - This improves your ability to block face detection.
- **Develop an asymmetrical look** - Facial-recognition algorithms expect symmetry between the left and right sides of the face.

Cyber Recovery Plan - Provides guidance to building maintenance personnel when responding to an intentional cyber-attack on a BCS. Instructs personnel on documenting the nature and scope of the cyber-attack. Prepared to instruct the *Incident Response Team* how to restore normal building operations without triggering further damage.

Cyber Safety - Being online exposes us to cyber criminals and others who commit identity theft, fraud, and harassment. Every time we connect to the Internet—at home, at school, at work, or on our mobile devices—we make decisions that affect our cybersecurity. The proliferation of child predators using the Internet to target young victims has become a national crisis. A study showed that one in seven children will be solicited for sex online in the next year. SOURCE: DHS

Cybersecurity Framework Core - Identify, Protect, Detect, Respond, and Recover. SOURCE: NIST

Cyber-Squatting - Cyber-squatting entails registering a *domain name* to gain monetary benefit from a trademark that belongs to someone else. The domains are often used to redirect the victim to various scams including phishing email campaigns, pay-per-click ads and for-profit survey sites or more nefarious content such as ransomware or other forms of drive-by malware. *Crackers* create these fake websites such as for banks to fool customers into thinking they're clicking on their bank's legitimate website. Also, called *domain squatting*.

Cyberwarfare - Actions by a nation-state to penetrate another nation's computers or networks for the purposes of causing damage or disruption. The fifth domain of warfare (the others are: land, sea, air, and space). Cyberwarfare involves the use and targeting of computers and networks in warfare between nations or non-state actors, such as terrorist groups, political or ideological extremist groups, hacktivists, and transnational criminal organizations. It involves both offensive and defensive operations pertaining to the threat of *cyber-attacks*, *espionage* and *sabotage*. Offensive operations are expected to play a role in officially declared wars. *Foreign Policy Magazine* puts the size of China's "hacker army" at anywhere from 50,000 to 100,000 individuals. Although to date cyberwarfare has been limited to attacking information and communications networks, the possibility exists for *cyber-attacks* against computer-controlled equipment capable of causing harm and even death to a nation's civilian population.

The Laws and Customs of War on Land (Hague IV 1907) serve as a rule of conduct for belligerents and in their relations with inhabitants. It does not cover all the circumstances that may arise, however the signatories did not intend that unforeseen cases should be left to the judgment of military commanders. Signatories declared that inhabitants (non-combatants) and the belligerents remain under the protection and the rule of the principles of the law of nations, the laws of humanity, and the dictates of the public conscience. Article 3 states a belligerent party that violates the Regulations shall be responsible for all acts committed by persons forming part of its armed forces. The belligerent party being a Nation.

In accordance with the Annex to the Geneva Convention, Regulations Respecting the Laws and Customs of War on Land, the right of belligerents to adopt means of injuring the enemy is not unlimited. The laws, rights, and duties of war apply not only to armies, but also to militia and volunteer corps commanded by a person responsible for his subordinates. The Martens Clause was included in the preamble to the 1899 Hague Convention II and slightly modified in 1907. It is a longstanding and binding rule of International Humanitarian Law that specifically demands the application of "the principle of humanity" in armed conflict. Cyberwarfare is no exception. In 1863, General Orders No. 100: The Lieber Code, Article 22 stated, "The unarmed citizen is to be spared in person, property, and honor as much as the exigencies of war will admit."

Dancing Frog - *Hackerspeak* for a problem that occurs on a computer that will not reappear while anyone else is watching. SOURCE: The Jargon File (version 4.4.7)

Dangerous File Extensions - The .exe file extension isn't the only dangerous file extension to look out for. Files ending with these file extensions can also run code on your system, making them dangerous, too:

.bat, .cmd, .com, .lnk, .pif, .scr, .vb, .vbe, .vbs, .wsh, the .jar file extension can also be dangerous, as it will launch Java programs.

Dark-Emitting Diode (DED) - Hackerspeak for a burned-out LED. SOURCE: The Jargon File (version 4.4.7)

Dark Web - Dark web is the World Wide Web content that exists on darknets, overlay networks which use the public Internet but require specific software, configurations or authorization to access. Identities and locations of dark web users stay anonymous and cannot be tracked due to a layered encryption system. Dark web encryption technology routes users' data through a large number of intermediate servers to protect the users' identity and guarantee anonymity making it useful for cybercrime. *Cracker*s have been known to sell their services there individually or as a part of groups. The dark web forms a small part of the deep web, the part of the Web not indexed by search engines, and sometimes the term "deep web" is mistakenly used to refer specifically to the dark web. Tor ("The Onion Router") and I2P ("Invisible Internet Project") are good examples of the dark web.

Data Aggregation - Compilation of individual data systems and data that could result in the totality of the information being classified, or classified at a higher level, or of beneficial use to an adversary. SOURCE: CNSSI-4009

Data Execution Prevention (DEP) - DEP is a *Windows* security feature that can help prevent damage to your computer from viruses and other security threats. Harmful programs can try to attack Windows by attempting to execute code from your computer's memory reserved for Windows and other authorized programs. These types of attacks can harm your programs and files. DEP can help protect your computer by monitoring your programs to make sure that they use computer memory safely. If DEP notices a program on your computer using memory incorrectly, it closes the program and notifies you. You can turn DEP off entirely or for a trusted program.

DAU (Dümmster Anzunehmender User) - German acronym for stupidest imaginable user. A cretin, fool, loser and weasel.

Death Code - *Hackerspeak* for a routine whose job is to set everything in the computer — registers, memory, flags, everything — to zero, including that portion of memory where it is running; it's last act is to stomp on its own "*store zero*" instruction. Death code isn't very useful, but writing it is seen as an interesting hacking challenge. SOURCE: The Jargon File (version 4.4.7)

Decoy Document - In a *phishing* attack, an exploit email prompts the target to open a **.src** file, display a decoy document to the user and executes the malware on the victim's device.

Deep Magic - *Hackerspeak* for an awesomely arcane technique central to a program or system, esp. one neither generally published nor available to hackers at large; one that could only have been composed by a true Wizard. Compiler optimization techniques and many aspects of OS design used to be deep magic; many techniques in cryptography, signal processing, graphics, and especially AI and neural networks still are. SOURCE: The Jargon File (version 4.4.7)

Deep Space - *Hackerspeak* for any program that has gone off the trolley. A program that just sits there silently grinding long after either failure or some output is expected. SOURCE: The Jargon File (version 4.4.7)

Deep Web - The part of the Web not indexed by search engines. Sometimes the term "*deep web*" is mistakenly used to refer specifically to the "*dark web*".

Deflicted - *Hackerspeak* for hardware that is broken due to poor design or shoddy manufacturing or both. SOURCE: The Jargon File (version 4.4.7)

Deletia - *Hackerspeak* for material omitted from the quote of the original email reply. Usually written rather than spoken; often appears as a pseudo-tag or ellipsis in the body of the reply, as "[deletia]" or "<deletia>" or "<snip>". SOURCE: The Jargon File (version 4.4.7)

Demon Dialer - *Hackerspeak* for a program which repeatedly calls the same telephone number. Demon dialing may be used as a prank or denial-of-service attack. SOURCE: The Jargon File (version 4.4.7)

Device Description Language (DDL) - The formal language describing the service and configuration of *field devices* for process and factory automation. *Field devices* for process and factory automation have a number of configuration options, to customize them to their individual use case. For these means they are equipped with a digital communication interface. Different software tools provide the means to control and configure the devices. In the 1990s, the DDL was developed to remove the requirement to write a new software tool for each new device type. Software can, through the interpretation of a device description (DD), configure and control many different devices. The creation of a description with the DDL is less effort than writing an entire software tool. Also, see *Electronic Device Description Language* and *Field Device Tool*.

Dictionary Flame - *Hackerspeak* for an attempt to sidetrack a debate away from issues by insisting on meanings for key terms that presuppose a desired conclusion or smuggle in an implicit premise. A common tactic of people who prefer argument over definitions to disputes about reality. SOURCE: The Jargon File (version 4.4.7)

Digital Trail - Here is a sample of the digital trail that can be mined: trace mobile phone location via *geo-tagging* (geographical *meta data* can divulge the longitude and latitude of the target), track the location of the target phone at various times of the day and saved as target's *location history*, trace the *exact route* the target phone has taken from one location to another, receive alert notification through SMS, email or both if the target phone enters restricted areas, receive a notification if the target phone leaves an area marked as "*safe*", know when the target is going somewhere they shouldn't be going, *listen to phone calls* live, record calls, view *call history*, view *Facebook* chats, view *Skype* chats, view *iMessage* chats, view *BBM chats*, listen to and *record phone surroundings*, view web *browser history*, view *bookmarks*, read target's *sent/receive emails*, view target's email *contacts* list, view target's *address book*, view *calendar entries*, look at meeting scheduler, view *task logs*, look at location history to find out travel routes, remotely *control cell phone*, *lock phone*, *erase all memory* on phone, view installed *apps*, view *SMS messages*, view send and receive SMS, view deleted SMS, redirect SMS, *view multimedia* files, get access to *photos*, watch *videos* files, listen to *audio* files, view *alerts and notifications*, receive alerts on SIM change, receive alerts on use of *specific numbers and words*, receive *alert when cell phone battery is removed* (indicating target does not want to be tracked), track *On-Star* vehicle location.

Digital Tunnel - A link between two locations through encryption of all traffic to add security to the connection.

Digital Twin - A digital copy of an asset is used to perform simulation, testing, and optimization in a virtual environment before committing actual resources. This virtual asset can include an archive of historical and real-time data, drawings, models, bills of material, engineering and dimensional analysis, manufacturing data, and operational history that can be used as a baseline to benchmark performance.

Dirty Power - Electrical mains voltage that is unfriendly to the delicate hardware in computers. Spikes, drop-outs, average voltage significantly higher or lower than nominal, or just plain noise can all cause problems of varying subtlety and severity.

Disappearing Malware - Malware that resides only in the infected machine's random-access-memory, rather than on the hard drive, so that the malware leaves no discernible footprint once it's gone. A *fileless malware attack* is similar because no malware gets installed on the system and the *cracker* uses the existing legitimate tools on the machine such as *Microsoft Powershell* or *WMI*. Tracking *fileless* attacks is difficult, but not impossible using memory forensics techniques.

Disappearing Message - A feature that allows users to let messages self-destruct in as little as five seconds or as long as a week.

Discretionary Access Control (DAC) - A type of access control defined by the *Trusted Computer System Evaluation Criteria* "as a means of restricting access to objects based on the identity of subjects and/or groups to which they belong. The controls are discretionary in the sense that a subject with a certain access permission is capable of passing that permission (perhaps indirectly) on to any other subject (unless restrained by mandatory access control)". Discretionary access control is commonly discussed in contrast to *mandatory access control* (MAC, sometimes termed *non-discretionary access control*). Occasionally a system as a whole is said to have "discretionary" or "purely discretionary" access control as a way of saying that the system lacks mandatory access control. On the other hand, systems can be said to implement both MAC and DAC simultaneously, where DAC refers to one category of access controls that subjects can transfer among each other, and MAC refers to a second category of access controls that imposes constraints upon the first. Also, something the user can manage, such as a document's password.

Distance Bounding - This is a technique that can be used for smartphone location verification in order to mitigate *location spoofing*. A nearby *Wi-Fi access point* can collaborate with the *location client* app in a smartphone to verify that the phone is in a location that it claims to be in. It takes advantage of the physical limitations of wireless technologies to deduce and verify the location of a particular smartphone. Another location verification technique is based on network latency measurements by comparing the latency (round-trip) time to a client with other known reference points.

Distributed Control System (DCS) - A *DCS* is a computerized control system for a process or plant, in which *autonomous controllers* are distributed throughout the system, but there is central operator supervisory control. This is in contrast to *non-distributed control systems* that use *centralized controllers*; either discrete controllers located at a central control room or within a central computer. DCS are dedicated systems used in manufacturing processes that are continuous or batch-oriented. *DCS* uses *function blocks* (self-contained "*blocks*" of code that emulate analog hardware control components and perform tasks essential to process control, such as execution of *PID algorithms*). *DCS* increases reliability and reduces installation costs by localizing control functions near the process plant, but enables monitoring and supervisory control of the process remotely. *SCADA* and *DCS* systems are very similar, but *DCS* is used where *high reliability* and *security* is important because of the distribution of the control processing around nodes in the system. If a single processor fails, it will only affect one section of the plant process, as opposed to a failure of a central computer which would affect the whole process. DCSs in *very high reliability* applications can have *dual redundant processors* with "hot" switch over on fault, to enhance the reliability of the control system. As wireless protocols are developed and refined, DCS increasingly includes wireless communication. *DCS* controllers are now often equipped with *embedded servers* and provide on-the-go *web access*. Many vendors provide the option of a mobile *HMI*, ready for both *Android* and *iOS*. With these interfaces, the threat of security breaches and possible damage to plant and process are now very real.

Disusered - *Hackerspeak* for a person whose account on a computer has been removed, esp. for cause rather than through normal attrition. SOURCE: The Jargon File (version 4.4.7)

Double Extensions - Files with names with double extensions are in most cases malicious files (*malware*). *Crackers* use this trick to make a file look like something it's not. Since windows hides extensions by default, they can make a file look like a text document, whereas it actually could be a .exe file. For example, "Test.txt.exe" (without quotes) would appear thusly on the screen: Test.txt Also, see *Unitrix Exploit.*

Drunk Mouse Syndrome - A malady exhibited by the mouse pointing device. The typical symptom is for the mouse cursor on the screen to move in random directions and not in sync with the motion of the actual mouse. SOURCE: The Jargon File (version 4.4.7)

Dust Explosion - This is the rapid combustion of fine particles suspended in the air, often but not always in an enclosed location. Dust explosions can occur where any dispersed powdered combustible material is present in high enough concentrations in the atmosphere or other oxidizing gaseous medium such as oxygen. Dust explosions may be classified as being either "*primary*" or "*secondary*" in nature. *Primary* dust explosions may occur inside process equipment or similar enclosures, and are generally controlled by pressure relief through purpose-built ducting to the external atmosphere. *Secondary* dust explosions are the result of dust accumulation inside a building being disturbed and ignited by the primary explosion, resulting in a much more dangerous uncontrolled explosion inside the workplace. Historically, fatalities from dust explosions have largely been the result of secondary dust explosions. When a dust explosion occurs, especially in a confined space such as a warehouse or silo, a significant increase in pressure is created, often more than sufficient to demolish the structure. Even materials that are traditionally thought of as nonflammable (such as aluminum), or slow burning (such as wood), can produce a powerful explosion when finely divided, and can be ignited by even a small spark. Areas subject to such dangers commonly maintain *very high air humidity* to reduce the chance of *dust explosions.*

Egosurf - *Hackerspeak* for someone searching the net for their name or links to their web pages. SOURCE: The Jargon File (version 4.4.7)

Electronic Device Description Language (EDDL) - EDDL is an international standard (IEC 61804). EDDL technology is used by major manufacturers to describe the information that is accessible in intelligent field devices. *Electronic Device Descriptions (EDDs)* are available for millions of devices that are currently installed in the process industry. The technology is used by the major process control systems and maintenance tool suppliers to support device diagnostics and calibration. Also, see *Field Device Tool.*

Electronic Health Records (EHR) - Hospitals rely heavily on a clinical data warehouse, translational bioinformatics, clinical informatics, health information systems, and patient records. A *cracker* that can access electronic health records can alter the data to cause physicians to *misdiagnose, prescribe the wrong drugs, administer unwarranted treatment* of cause the patient to *forego needed treatment.*

Embedded Web Server - Web server software built into a building control system field device that is provided to configure the device from a web browser. Also, used remotely by equipment vendors to update software or troubleshoot problems. The low-powered hardware-centric nature of *embedded systems* presents them with unique security threats. Protocols like *CoAP (Constrained Application Protocol)* are specifically designed for brokerless *Machine-to-Machine* communication in low power environments.

Below are three *anti-patterns* that have been used by real *Internet-of-Things* devices:

HTTP Pub/Sub
If you want your coffee machine to brew some coffee every time your IoT-enabled alarm clock sounds, your coffee machine subscribes to messages published by your alarm clock to implement the *Publish/Subscribe Pattern* within the *API* of the IoT devices. An attacker with the ability to set subscriptions on the alarm clock can send *HTTP* messages to any device or Internet property and if done across enough devices, a *DDOS* vulnerability is created.

TLS
Some IoT developers are implementing TLS to secure communications on IoT devices and running devices themselves as web servers and using self-signed server-side certificates to encrypt such requests. This poses a security risk by failing to maintain trust relationships. In place of this; devices can communicate through brokers; such brokers can act as web servers with a signed TLS certificates installed server-side which can be authenticated.

Unencrypted Bootloader
IoT devices are located in insecure environments - as such extra precautions need to be taken to protect the memory on such a device. A stolen device can be *reverse-engineered* to extract software from the embedded system chip running on it. A solution to this is to encrypt the *bootloaders* on such devices using *Hardware-based Key Storage* such as *Atmel*'s *CryptoAuthentication* chips and *Microchip*'s PIC24F GB2 microcontroller.
SOURCE: Cloud Flare Blog

Embedded Systems - An embedded system is a computer system with a dedicated function within a larger mechanical or electrical system, often with real-time computing constraints. It is embedded as part of a complete device often including hardware and mechanical parts. Embedded systems control many devices in common use today. Ninety-eight percent of all microprocessors are manufactured as components of embedded systems.

Energy Management Controls System (EMCS) - A *Building Automation System* designed to enhance energy-efficiency. This device can be tampered with and shut down the entire building. It can also be reprogrammed to very high light levels and waste energy.

Enhancement - *Hackerspeak* for a bug fix. A hacker being ironic would instead call the fix a feature — or perhaps save some effort by declaring the bug itself to be a feature. SOURCE: The Jargon File (version 4.4.7)

Exabyte - One quintillion bytes. Equivalent to 1000 petabytes = 1 million terabytes = 1 billion gigabytes. exa indicates multiplication by the sixth power of 1000 (10^{18}). The symbol for the exabyte is EB.

Exbibyte - A multiple of the unit byte for digital information (binary). The prefix exbi (symbol Ei) represents multiplication by 2^{60}, therefore: 1 exbibyte = 2^{60} bytes = 1152921504606846976 bytes = 1024 pebibytes The exbibyte is closely related to the exabyte (EB). One exbibyte (1 EiB) is approximately equal to 1.15 EB. Its unit symbol is EiB.

Explosionproof Enclosures - Solid cabinets that contain different electrical components like switches, plugs, sockets, transformers, controls, and knobs to keep the surroundings safe from electrical hazards. Integrated with sound technology, these boxes are resistant to spark and shock and have a high tolerance to extreme temperatures. An ideal solution for hazardous locations; these explosion-proof enclosures keep any interior explosion from spreading to the external environment and damaging life and property.

Eyeball Search - *Hackerspeak* to look for something in a mass of code or data with one's own native optical sensors, as opposed to using some sort of *pattern matching software* like *grep* or any other automated search tool. SOURCE: The Jargon File (version 4.4.7)

Face Recognition App - Face recognition is one way being tried to use biometrics for authentication. Lloyds Bank will trial *Microsoft's Windows Hello* technology, which lets online users log into their web-based accounts by pointing their face at a computer's *webcam*. *Windows Hello* uses infra-red sensors to build a reliable representation of a human face. *Microsoft* says the technology can't be fooled by holding up a photograph to the lens. Reports have surfaced that the facial-recognition feature of *Samsung*'s new *Galaxy S8 smartphone* could be tricked exactly that way.

Failure Alarms - Derived failure alarms combine inputs from multiple alarm points into a single, software-configured alarm, using simple Boolean logic. A *low battery* is a *MINOR* alarm. *Low battery* AND an *AC power failure* OR *generator failure* is a *MAJOR* alarm, but a *low battery* AND *AC power failure* AND *backup generator failure* is a *CRITICAL* alarm. If a failure alarm is remotely disabled by a *cracker* it would be impossible to know when a device is not working properly.

Fake Websites - *Crackers* can deceive users into handing over personal details or login information by using domains disguised as legitimate websites by *cyber-squatting*. To avoid falling for a fake website, consumers should:
- Check for extra added letters in the domain, such as Gooogle.com
- Check for dashes in the domain name, such as Face-book.com
- Look out for "**rn**" disguised as an "**m**", such as mode**m**.com versus mode**rn**.com
- Check for reversed letters, such as Y**uo**tube.com
- A plural or singular form of the domain, such as Domaintool.com

Farm - *Hackerspeak* for a group of machines, especially a large group of near-identical machines running load-balancing software, dedicated to a single task. Example: a server farm. SOURCE: The Jargon File (version 4.4.7)

FAULT_OUT_OF_RANGE - Detects whether the monitored value is outside the range of values considered to be normal for the object. A *cracker* can disable this signal allowing monitored values to exceed design limits, possibly causing severe damage to equipment.

Feature Shock - *Hackerspeak* for a user's confusion when confronted with a package that has too many features and poor introductory material. SOURCE: The Jargon File (version 4.4.7)

Field Circus - *Hackerspeak* for the *field service* organization of any hardware manufacturer. There is an entire genre of jokes about field circus engineers:

Q: How can you recognize a field circus engineer with a flat tire?
A: He's changing one tire at a time to see which one is flat.
SOURCE: The Jargon File (version 4.4.7)

Field Device Integration (FDI) - An effort to integrate the two technologies used for presenting and managing information from intelligent devices: *Field Device Tool* (FDT) and *Electronic Device Description Language* (EDDL) to form a single solution. Both technologies are complementary in some ways and overlap in other ways. FDI promises a common set of development tools and a single path to managing the flood of information from intelligent devices across different networks to the applications that need it. All the major suppliers support both FDT and EDDL technology. FDI technology allows any enabled device to be accessed from any compliant host using any field communication protocol.

Field Device Tool (FDT) - FDT is accepted as IEC 62453 and supports over 16 protocols used in both process and factory automation, including *FOUNDATION* fieldbus, *HART* and *PROFIBUS*. FDT can do some advanced functions that EDDL cannot do, such as graphical representation of information. The essential parts of FDT technology are the *frame application* (FDT Frame) and *Device Type Managers* (Device DTM and CommDTM), which are available for field devices and communication equipment. The two components are similar to the *Print Manager* in a *Windows Office* program and the *Print Drivers* and their associated *GUI* that must be installed to make printers work.

File-Renaming Tricks - *Crackers* sometimes use file name tricks to get victims to execute malicious code such as naming the file something that would encourage unsuspecting victims to click on it. *Microsoft Windows* readily hides common file extensions, so a file named *NudePics.Gif.exe* is displayed as *NudePics.Gif*.

Fingerprint Scan Logon - *Microsoft's Outlook, Xbox, Skype*, and other cloud-based users can now log on with a fingerprint scan on their smartphone. Soon users will be able to take their phone, walk up to a *Windows 10* PC and just use a thumb print to log in.

Firmware Validation Bypass Vulnerability - A scenario where a *cracker* replaces the legitimate firmware of a *SCADA* or *BCS* device with a malicious one in a ransomware attack. The attacker connects to the targeted device's interface, creates a backup for the configuration of the targeted device, and installs firmware that disrupts regular processes. In order to prevent the victim from restoring the firmware, the *cracker* will disable the firmware and *configuration update* functionality. The *restore factory settings* feature does not mitigate the attack in most cases as the process does not restore the original firmware, and this feature can also be disabled by a *cracker*.

Fireworks Mode - *Hackerspeak* for the mode a machine is sometimes said to be in when it is performing a crash and burn operation. SOURCE: The Jargon File (version 4.4.7)

Firmware - *Hackerspeak* differs from straight *techspeak* in that *hackers* don't normally apply firmware to stuff that you can't possibly get at, such as the program that runs a pocket calculator. Instead, it implies that the firmware could be changed, even if doing so would mean opening a box and plugging in a new chip. A computer's *BIOS* is the classic example. SOURCE: The Jargon File (version 4.4.7)

Flammability Limit - Mixtures of dispersed combustible materials (such as gaseous or vaporized fuels, and some dusts) and air will burn only if the fuel concentration lies within well-defined lower and upper bounds determined experimentally, referred to as flammability limits or explosive limits. Combustion can range in violence from *deflagration*, through *detonation*, to *explosion*. Limits vary with temperature and pressure, but are normally expressed in terms of volume percentage at 25 °C and atmospheric pressure. These limits are relevant both to producing and optimizing explosion or combustion, as in an engine, or to preventing it, as in uncontrolled explosions of build-ups of combustible gas or dust.

Flytrap - *Hackerspeak* for a firewall machine. SOURCE: The Jargon File (version 4.4.7)

Footprinting - In the case of a hospital cyber-attack, this is how the *cracker* starts his analysis of the target network. The *cracker* sifts through *open-source* material found on the *Internet* to learn all he can about the hospital including who works there, what equipment is there, and where it is located. A *cracker* may visit the hospital, *sniff* the wireless spectrum, look in dumpsters, and use *social engineering* to assemble a very good picture of the hospital and its *active medical device*s to determine where the vulnerabilities are and how best to attack. Once the *cracker* knows who manufactured the device he intends to attack, he will find a copy of the operating and maintenance manuals (many are available on-line). Unfortunately, those manuals usually reveal the *default password* set at the factory. And, to make matters worse, some manufacturers recommend you not change the *default password* to make it easier for the vendor to do remote diagnostics on the equipment!

Fractionating Column - Fractionating columns are used for large-scale industrial distillations and in small scale laboratory distillations to separate a mixture into its component parts, or fractions, by helping the mixed vapors to cool, condense, and vaporize again, based on the differences in volatilities. Fractionating columns are widely used in the chemical process industries where large quantities of liquids have to be distilled. Industrial distillation is typically performed in large, vertical cylindrical columns known as *distillation towers* or *distillation columns.* The amount of *heat* entering a distillation column is a *crucial operating parameter*, addition of excess or insufficient heat to the column can lead to *foaming, weeping, entrainment*, or *flooding.* If the column contains liquid during pressuring, caution must be exercised as excessive vapor flows may cause flooding and *gas lifting* of the liquid, resulting in liquid discharge into relief header and possible damage to column internals.

Fritterware - *Hackerspeak* for an excess of capability that serves no productive end. Anything that eats huge amounts of time for quite marginal gains in function, but seduces people into using it anyway. SOURCE: The Jargon File (version 4.4.7)

Functional Manufacturing Levels - The functional manufacturing levels using computerized control. Levels 1 and 2 are the functional levels of a traditional DCS, in which all equipment are part of an integrated system from a single manufacturer. Levels 3 and 4 are not strictly process control in the traditional sense, but where production control and scheduling takes place.
- **Level 0** contains the field devices such as flow and temperature sensors, and final control elements, such as control valves
- **Level 1** contains the industrialized Input/Output (I/O) modules, and their associated distributed electronic processors.
- **Level 2** contains the supervisory computers, which collect information from processor nodes on the system, and provide the operator control screens.
- **Level 3** is the production control level, which does not directly control the process, but is concerned with monitoring production and monitoring targets
- **Level 4** is the production scheduling level.

Full Recovery Test - An exercise in which all recovery procedures and strategies are tested (as opposed to a Partial Recovery Test.)

Fusible Plug - A fusible plug operates as a safety valve when dangerous *temperatures*, rather than dangerous pressures, are reached in a closed vessel.

Fuzzing - *Fuzzing* or *fuzz testing* is an automated software testing technique that involves providing invalid, unexpected, or random data as inputs to a computer program. The program is then monitored for exceptions such as crashes, or failing built-in code assertions or for finding potential memory leaks. Typically, *fuzzers* are used to test programs that take structured inputs. This structure is specified, e.g., in a file format or protocol and distinguishes valid from invalid input. An effective *fuzzer* generates semi-valid inputs that are "valid enough" so that they are not directly rejected from the parser, but able to exercise interesting behaviors deeper in the program and "invalid enough" so that they might stress different corner cases and expose errors in the parser. For the purpose of security, input that crosses a trust boundary is often the most interesting. For example, it is more important to fuzz code that handles the upload of a file by any user than it is to *fuzz* the code that parses a configuration file that is accessible only to a privileged user.

/GS (Buffer Security Check) - *Visual Studio* feature that detects some buffer overruns that overwrite a function's return address, exception handler address, or certain types of parameters. Causing a buffer overrun is a technique used by *crackers* to exploit code that does not enforce buffer size restrictions. /GS is on by default.

GAU (Größter Anzunehmender Unfall) - German from the engineering-slang for *worst credible accident* or something with similarly disastrous consequences. In popular German, *GAU* is used only to refer to *worst-case* nuclear accidents such as a core meltdown.

Geek Code - *Hackerspeak* for a set of codes commonly used in sig blocks to broadcast the interests, skills, and aspirations of the poster. Features a G at the left margin followed by numerous letter codes, often suffixed with plusses or minuses. Also, called *"Code of the Geeks"*. SOURCE: The Jargon File (version 4.4.7)

Genius From Mars Technique - *Hackerspeak* for a visionary quality which enables one to ignore the standard approach and come up with a totally unexpected new algorithm. An attack on a problem from an offbeat angle that no one has ever thought of before, but that in retrospect makes total sense. SOURCE: The Jargon File (version 4.4.7)

Geo-Fence - A *geo-fence* is a virtual perimeter defined by *GPS* or *RFID* technology, for a real-world geographic area. A *geo-fence* could be dynamically generated—as in a radius around a store or point location, or a geo-fence can be a predefined set of boundaries, like school attendance zones or neighborhood boundaries. The use of a geo-fence is called *geo-fencing*, and one example of usage involves a *location-aware device* of a *location-based service (LBS)* user entering or exiting a *geo-fence*. This activity could trigger an alert to the device's user as well as messaging to the geo-fence operator. This info, which could contain the location of the device, could be sent to a mobile telephone or an email account. Not only do some retailers put up a geofence around their building, some have been known to put geofences around a competitor's store, so then they know, out of their loyalty base, what customers also frequent their competitors' businesses.

Geomessaging - Geomessaging is a technology that allows a system to send a message based on any media to a *location-aware device* that enters or exits a *geo-fenced* area. Those areas can be created by using *geofences*, based on Latitude and Longitude, or adding *beacons* to the system associating those beacons with named locations. The device will receive the message according to a predefined set of rules.

Gh0st RAT - Chinese-created *Remote Access Tool* (malware) that has been used for cyber-crimes since 2009.

Ghosting - This is the problem that some keyboard keys don't work when multiple keys are pressed simultaneously. The key presses that don't show up on the computer or seem to have disappeared are said to have been *"ghosted."* On most keyboards, even some that are explicitly marketed as *"Anti-Ghosting,"* this happens with many three key combinations.

Gibibyte - A multiple of the unit byte for digital information (binary). The binary prefix gibi means 2^{30}, therefore one gibibyte is equal to 1073741824 bytes = 1024 mebibytes. One GB is defined by the IEC as 10^9 bytes = 1000000000bytes, 1GiB $\approx$ 1.074GB. 1024 gibibytes are equal to one tebibyte. The unit symbol for the gibibyte is GiB.

GitHub - A web-based version control repository and Internet hosting service. It provides access control and collaboration features such as bug tracking, feature requests, task management, and wikis for every project.

Glark - *Hackerspeak* refers to figure something out from context. "The System III manuals are pretty poor, but you can generally *glark* the meaning from context." Interestingly, the word was originally '*glork*'; but hacker usage mutated the verb to '*glark*' because *glork* was already an established jargon term (some hackers do report using the original term). SOURCE: The Jargon File (version 4.4.7)

Glork - *Hackerspeak* refers to term of mild surprise, usually tinged with outrage, as when one attempts to save the results of two hours of editing and finds that the system has just crashed.

Goober with Firewall (GWF) - *Hackerspeak* refers to a *luser* who has equipped his desktop computer with a hypersensitive "software firewall" or host intrusion detection program, and who gives its alerts absolute credence. ISP tech support and *abuse desks* dread hearing from such persons, who insist that every packet of abnormal traffic the software detects is "a *cracker*".

Go Flatline - *Hackerspeak* when a machine dies, terminates, or fails irreversibly. This is used of machines only; human death being considered somewhat too serious a matter to employ jargon-jokes about. SOURCE: The Jargon File (version 4.4.7)

Goat File - A sacrificial file used to test a computer virus, i.e. a *dummy executable* that carries a sample of the virus, isolated so it can be studied. Not common among hackers.

Godzillagram - *Hackerspeak* for a network packet that in theory is a broadcast to every machine in the universe. The typical case is an *IP datagram* whose destination IP address is [255.255.255.255]. Fortunately, few *gateways* are foolish enough to attempt to implement this case. A network packet of maximum size. An IP *Godzillagram* has 65,535 octets. SOURCE: The Jargon File (version 4.4.7)

Google Brillo - See *Android Things*.

Google Is Your Friend (GIYF) - *Hackerspeak* used to suggest, gently and politely, that you have just asked a question of human beings that would have been better directed to a search engine. Also, referred to as *STFW (Search The Fucking Web)*.

Google Juice - *Hackerspeak* for a hypothetical substance which attracts the index bots of Google.com. In common usage, a web page or web site with high placement in the results of a particular search on *Google* or frequent placement in the results of a various searches is said to have "a lot of google juice" or "good google juice". Also, used to compare web pages or web sites, for example "CrackMonkey has more google juice than KPMG". SOURCE: The Jargon File (version 4.4.7)

Graphical User Interface (GUI) - The graphical display consists of building system (air handler units, VAV boxes, chillers, cooling towers, boilers, etc.) graphic displays. Data associated with an active display is updated every 5 seconds. Each Building or Building Sub-Area display shows the building foot print and basic floor plan, and distinguishes between the individual zones and the equipment serving each zone and space. The building display shows all space sensor and status readings, as applicable, for the individual zones such as space temperature, humidity, occupancy status, etc. The building display also shows the locations of individual pieces of monitored and controlled equipment. Also referred to as a graphical user interface. Hack into this and you can send false signals that everything is working fine or that things that are working properly are not operating properly.

Green Machine - *Hackerspeak* for a computer or peripheral device that has been designed and built to *military specifications* for field equipment (to withstand mechanical shock, extremes of temperature and humidity). Comes from the olive-drab 'uniform' paint used for military equipment. SOURCE: The Jargon File (version 4.4.7)

Greyball - This a software tool used by the ride-hailing service *Uber* to identify and deny service to certain riders including law enforcement. *Greyball* used several methods to identify and deny service to government officials who were investigating *Uber* for violations of local laws. Those methods included:
- **Geofencing**. Uber would create a digital map that identified the locations of city government offices. If a potential rider attempted to hail a ride from the area around a government building, *Greyball* would flag the individual as a possible *law enforcement* agent.
- **Mining credit card databases**. If *Uber* identified a credit card as being associated with a government agency or police union, it would flag that individual in *Greyball*.
- **Identifying devices**. Since government agencies would often buy *cheap cellphones* for use in *sting operations*, *Uber* employees would visit electronics stores to obtain *model numbers for inexpensive phones* and input those model numbers into *Greyball*.

- **Searches of social media**. *Uber* employees searched *social media profiles* to identify possible *law enforcement agents*. Uber then flagged those individuals in *Greyball*.
- **Eyeballing**. *Greyball* would determine if a potential rider had been opening and closing the *Uber* app numerous times without calling for a ride.

Gweep - *Hackerspeak* meaning to hack, usually at night. SOURCE: The Jargon File (version 4.4.7)

Hack Mode - *Hackerspeak* for what one is in when hacking. Some aspects of hacker etiquette will appear quite odd to an observer unaware of the high value placed on hack mode. For example, if someone appears at your door, it is perfectly okay to hold up a hand (without turning one's eyes away from the screen) to avoid being interrupted. One may read, type, and interact with the computer for quite some time before further acknowledging the other's presence (of course, he or she is reciprocally free to leave without a word). The understanding is that you might be in hack mode and you dare not swap that context out until you have reached a good point to pause. SOURCE: The Jargon File (version 4.4.7)

Hackattack - *Hackerspeak* for a hack session extended long outside normal working times, especially one longer than 12 hours. Nearly synonymous with *hacking run*, though the latter more strongly implies an all-nighter. May cause you to *change phase* the hard way (stay awake for a very long time in order to get into a different *phase*). SOURCE: The Jargon File (version 4.4.7)

Hacker Ethic - *Hackerspeak* referring to the belief that information-sharing is a powerful positive good, and that it is an ethical duty of hackers to share their expertise by writing open-source code and facilitating access to information wherever possible. The belief that system-cracking for fun and exploration is ethically OK as long as the *hacker* commits no theft, vandalism, or breach of confidentiality. Some hackers consider the act of cracking itself to be unethical, like breaking and entering. SOURCE: The Jargon File (version 4.4.7)

Hackintosh - A "fake" *Mac* built with standard PC components PC that runs *macOS*. Starting in 2006, all Macs are powered by the same *Intel CPUs* included in PCs. Also, called a *CustoMac*. SOURCE: TonyMacx86.com

HackRF - A USB-powered *Software Defined Radio* peripheral capable of transmission or reception of radio signals from 10 MHz to 6 GHz.

Halon - A toxic gas used to extinguish fires effective only in closed areas. Being phased out. If a *cracker* can release Halon into the server room, it can injure employees.

Halt and Catch Fire (HCF) - *Hackerspeak* for any of several undocumented and semi-mythical machine instructions with destructive side-effects, supposedly included for test purposes on several well-known architectures going as far back as the *IBM 360*. This instruction caused the processor to toggle a subset of the bus lines as rapidly as it could; in some configurations, this could actually cause lines to burn up. See *Killer Poke*. SOURCE: The Jargon File (version 4.4.7)

Heavy Wizardry - *Hackerspeak* for code or designs that trade on a particularly intimate knowledge or experience of a particular operating system or language or complex application interface. Distinguished from *deep magic*, which trades more on arcane theoretical knowledge. Writing *device drivers* is *heavy wizardry*. SOURCE: The Jargon File (version 4.4.7)

Heisenbug - *Hackerspeak* for a *bug* that disappears or alters its behavior when one attempts to probe or isolate it. SOURCE: The Jargon File (version 4.4.7)

High-Integrity Pressure Protection System (HIPPS) - HIPPS is a type of *safety instrumented system* (SIS) designed to prevent over-pressurization of a plant, such as a chemical plant or oil refinery. The HIPPS will shut off the source of the high pressure before the design pressure of the system is exceeded, thus preventing loss of containment through rupture (explosion) of a line or vessel. Therefore, a HIPPS is a barrier between a high-pressure and a low-pressure section of an installation. Whereas a pressure relief system is designed to provide an alternative outlet for removing any excess inflow of fluids for safe disposal, HIPPS aims at stopping the inflow of excess fluids and containing them in the system. A HIPPS closes the source of overpressure within 2 seconds with at least the same reliability as a safety relief valve.

Home Box - *Hackerspeak* for a hacker's personal machine. SOURCE: The Jargon File (version 4.4.7)

Home Security Systems - Historically, home security systems were hardwired to a service provider operations center, however today they are connected wirelessly. This allows a homeowner to monitor his home at all times, from anywhere, using a smartphone or tablet. It also makes it much easier to be hacked.

Hooking - Refers to techniques used to alter or augment the behavior of an operating system, of applications, or of other software components by intercepting function calls or messages or events passed between software components. Code that handles such intercepted function calls, events or messages is called a *hook*.

Hospital Insider Threats - Insider threat to a hospital's critical infrastructure is more serious than outsider threats because an outside attacker is less likely to know the hospital's network vulnerabilities and its weaknesses as well as an insider would. The behavioral characteristics of hospital employees are potential indicators and patterns to detect insider threat activity. No one behavior by itself would be an issue, but questionable behaviors are more likely to be manifested in multiple observables. A list of observable employee behavior to look for which could serve as precursors to malicious activity can be found in my book *"Cybersecurity for Hospitals and Healthcare Facilities"*.

Hot Site - An alternate facility that has the equipment and resources to recover the business functions affected by the occurrence of a disaster. Hot-sites may vary in type of facilities offered (such as data processing, communication, or any other critical business functions needing duplication). Location and size of the hot-site will be proportional to the equipment and resources needed. Similar Terms: *Backup site; Recovery site; Recovery Center; Alternate processing site*.

Hot Wallet - A *Bitcoin* wallet that is online and connected in some way to the Internet.

HTTPS Everywhere - A *Firefox, Chrome* and *Opera* web browser extension that encrypts your communications with many major websites, making your browsing more secure.

HyperFace - A textile pattern containing vaguely face-shaped assortments of pixels that form "ideal" face template images, as understood by the most commonly-used *face detection* method. This turns the material into a kind of camouflage, hiding the wearer's face by fooling the algorithm into detecting false ones.

ID-10-T error - *Hackerspeak* is a masked jab at the user: when *ID-Ten-T* is spelled out it becomes ID10T ("*IDIOT*"). Also, known as a "*Ten-T error*", "ID:10T error" and "ID107". Navy pronounces ID10T as "*Eye Dee Ten Tango*". Army pronounces 1D10T as "*One Delta Ten Tango*".

Industrial Control System (ICS) - An information system used to control industrial processes such as manufacturing, product handling, production, and distribution. Industrial control systems include *supervisory control and data acquisition systems (SCADA)* used to control geographically dispersed assets, as well as distributed control systems (DCS) and smaller control systems using programmable logic controllers to control localized processes. SOURCE: SP 800-53; SP 800-53A

Industrial Internet of Things (IIoT) - Application of the IoT for the manufacturing industry is called the IIoT (or *Industrial Internet* or *Industry 4.0*).

Industrial Robot Hacks - Researchers at *Trend Micro* and Italy's *Politecnico Milano* have demonstrated the risk of a networked and Internet-connected industrial robot. Cyber-attack techniques they developed were used to subtly sabotage and even fully hijack a 220-pound industrial robotic arm capable of wielding gripping claws, welding tools and lasers. The robotic arm they compromised has applications in everything from automotive manufacturing to food processing and packaging to pharmaceuticals. The researchers found a broad collection of security vulnerabilities in the controller computer that pilots that arm. Any remote attacker could use the Internet-scanning tool Shodan to find exposed, accessible FTP servers connected to the robots, and upload files to them that would be automatically downloaded and run whenever the robot is next rebooted. An attacker on the same network as the robot could use a flaw in its HTTP interface to cause it to run unauthorized commands, or broken the weak encryption the robot's controller used to protect its input data, allowing a *cracker* to subtly alter its parameters and it could then lie to the operator, even as the machine did the attacker's bidding. Researchers showed that the attack could subtly change manufacturing parameters and introduce imperceptible aberrations into the arm's movement that simply reduce its precision, altering a product by as a little as a few millimeters. The issues range from authentication problems to weak cryptography to insecure default software configurations. Since software updates for robots can often cause costly delays in manufacturing processes, factories often skip them. That means even known security flaws could linger in the robots for years.

Infrastructure - (1) The basic physical and organizational structures, facilities and utilities (e.g. roads, buildings, and water and power distribution systems) needed for the operation of a society. (2) The physical equipment (computers, cases, racks, cabling, etc.) that comprises a computer system; (3) the foundational basis that supports the information management capabilities, including the telecommunications and network connectivity. Hack into a community infrastructure and you can interrupt the day-to-day workings of an entire society.

Insider Attack - An entity inside the security perimeter that is authorized to access system resources, but uses them in a way not approved by those who granted the authorization. In addition to intentional violators, other types of insiders are:
  1. Exploited insiders may be "tricked" by external parties into providing data or passwords they shouldn't.
  2. Careless insiders may simply press the wrong key and accidentally delete or modify critical information.
  3. Malicious insiders intend to cause mischief, such as a disgruntled employee.

Insider Threat - The ability of a trusted insider to bypass or defeat security safeguards or otherwise adversely affect national security.

Institute of Electrical and Electronics Engineers (IEEE) - The largest technical society in the world, consisting of engineers, scientists, and students; has declared standards for computers and communications.

Internet Death Penalty (IDP) - *Hackerspeak* for the ultimate sanction against spam-emitting sites — complete shunning at the router level of all mail and packets, as well as *Usenet* messages, from the offending domain. SOURCE: The Jargon File (version 4.4.7)

Internet of (Hackable) Things - Easy-to-hack Internet-connected devices are taking over the world and the manufacturers of these hackable devices, who are spending all their time developing the next model rather than maintaining the old ones, probably don't care because they have nothing to lose—the *Internet of Things* has no anti-hacking safety standards or laws to comply with. Do we really need Internet connected air fresheners, toilet paper holders, and even jump ropes? It's funny now, but will you be laughing when a *cracker* breaks into your Internet-connected toilet-paper holder? How about rebooting the refrigerator?

Internet of Shit (IoS) - This started as an anonymous joke poking fun at the deluge of Internet-connected smart devices that sound like terrible ideas. Examples abound such as a $700 *WiFi*-connected juicer, a smart egg-minder, a cat-tracking water fountain, and a *Bluetooth* umbrella. The argument is that companies want to Internet-connect your entire house in order to *collect more data on you* that could eventually turn into *Software-as-a-Service* money-makers. Services that, eventually costs more than the initial cost of the device. *Nest* thermostat promises it "never stops learning" to make your heating better, because your data is valuable perpetually. That thing sits on your wall quietly observing without you knowing. *Nest* already shares "anonymous" data with "partners" and *Google* just happens to be in the business of showing you ads for things. The irony in all this is that crock-pots, light bulbs, thermostats, *GPS trackers* for kids, billboards, and even teddy bears have all been hacked recently. Who knew that a dishwasher connected to the Internet has a bug that allows hackers to break into it, infect it with *malware*, and give them the opportunity to use it as leverage to hack other devices on your network. Also, called the *Internet of Hackable Things*.

Internet of Things (IoT) - The network of physical objects or "things" embedded with electronics, software, sensors, and connectivity to enable devices to exchange data with other connected devices. The down side to all this is that the *IoT* can become a cheap tool for remote surveillance and reconnaissance and a great deal of information can be learned from device usage behavior. By aggregating this surveillance information about your building over time, an attacker could get a very accurate understanding of your building operations. According to *Motherboard Magazine*, there are already more than 6 billion "things" connected to the Internet, and there will be an estimated 20.8 billion by 2020. The billions of *IoT* devices are just waiting for the right *cracker* to come along and exploit their every weakness.

Internet tools such as *Wink* allow a person to control, from a single screen, his Internet-connected home devices, such as door locks, window shades and LED lights. Anyone capable of hacking your *Wink* account may be able to identify your social media accounts, the names of your devices (like Lou's *iPad*) and your network information. An app that monitors your grill's propane tank may record the tank's latitude and longitude, thus revealing the exact location of your house. Hacking into a *Nest* thermostat would allow someone to figure out when your house was occupied and when it was not. Manufacturers of *IP-enabled* devices say you can opt out of sharing information with vendors, software developers and third-party applications, but you may not be aware how much information their device is collecting. SOURCE: Wikipedia

Tor has taken a part in trying to help secure the *IoT*. By utilizing *Tors Onion Protocol*, vendors on the *IoT* will be able to easily use secure communications and securely update the delivery process for their devices. By using *Tor* along with the *IoT*, most of the angles of attack for smart devices can be eliminated.

The *European Union (EU)* is currently working on a sticker system of all Internet connected equipment. The EU commission wants to use stickers as a means to inform purchasers of the safety issues that could be associated with a device. The commission believes this type of regulatory system will give device manufacturers a push to create more secure devices. Higher security capable devices will be given permission to use a higher-class sticker.

Internetworks - An internetwork is a communication subsystem in which several networks are linked together to provide common data communication facilities that overlay the technologies and protocols of the individual component networks and the methods used for their interconnection. Internetworks are needed for the development of extensible, open distributed systems. The openness characteristic of distributed systems implies that the networks used in distributed systems should be extensible to very large numbers of computers, whereas individual networks have restricted address spaces and some may have performance limitations that are incompatible with their large-scale use. In internetworks, a variety of local and wide area network technologies can be integrated to provide the networking capacity needed by each group of users. Thus internetworks bring many of the benefits of open systems to the provision of communication in distributed systems.

Interoperability - The ability of one computer system to control another, even though the two systems are made by different manufacturers.

IoT Login Attempts - When you connect a controller to the Internet, expect the IP to be discovered quickly with login attempts beginning within 10 minutes. Most of it is automated and not an actual person trying to hack in.

So, if you have an open Telnet port (Port 23 or Port 2323) or an FTP port, make sure the password is unique and strong.

Iron Box - *Hackerspeak* for a special environment set up to trap a *cracker* logging in over remote connections long enough to be traced. May include a modified shell restricting the *cracker*'s movements in unobvious ways, and 'bait' files designed to keep him interested and logged on. SOURCE: The Jargon File (version 4.4.7)

ISMI Catcher - An electronic device that acts like a cell phone tower and tricks cell phones into interacting with them. They can be used to track a person's location, intercept data from phones including text and voice communications, instantly drain a target's batteries completely, and disrupt service. They are also known as *Stingray* and they have a range of one to two city blocks. *Stingrays* can interfere with cell phone service and some models can be used for blanketed or targeted denials of service.

Joe Code - *Hackerspeak* for code that is overly tense and unmaintainable. Badly written, possibly buggy code. SOURCE: The Jargon File (version 4.4.7)

Joe-Job - *Hackerspeak* referring to a spam run forged to appear as though it came from an innocent party, who is then generally flooded by the bounces; or, the act of performing such a run. SOURCE: The Jargon File (version 4.4.7)

Jump Box - A jump box is a "remote access server" used to provide access to critical assets inside an electronic security perimeter. The jump box is heavily defended - most services are turned off, most software un-installed, the box is fully patched, automatic-updated, anti-virus-ed, whitelisted/-HIPS'ed, anti-spyware-ed, host-firewalled and automatic-updated. The only port open to the enterprise network is the remote-control port, and you can defend that further with a VPN. The jump box is on a *DMZ* and you can control which hosts and services the jump box has access to on the critical network. Also, called a *jump server, jump host, jumpbox or secure administrative host.*

Keystone Computer Jack - Keystones are connection jacks that can snap into a faceplate so that an *RJ45* mod plug can be plugged into them.

KilerRat - A remote access trojan that can do such things as steal login credentials, manipulate the registry, and open a reverse shell, giving the attacker the capability to input commands directly into the system. It also can allow access to the victim's webcam. It is a variant of the well-known njrat.

Kill Switch -
(1) A *kill switch*, also known as an *emergency stop, e-stop*, and *Big Red Button*, is a safety mechanism used to shut off a device in an emergency situation in which it cannot be shut down in the usual manner. Unlike a normal shut-down switch/procedure, which shuts down all building control systems in an orderly fashion and turns the machine off without damaging it, a kill switch is designed and configured to completely and as quickly as possible abort the operation, *even if this damages equipment* and be operable in a manner that is quick, simple (so that even a panicking operator with impaired executive function can activate it), and, usually, be obvious even to an untrained operator or a bystander. In a *data center*, it is called a *scram switch*.
(2) A new definition for *kill switch* was revealed in regards to the recent *WannaCry virus* that infected thousands of computers worldwide in May 2017. *WannaCry* virus included a *sinkhole* test for a domain name that wasn't activated when the virus was propagating. As long as the virus found it was unable to connect to it, the virus would encrypt the target computer files and continue to try and infect other computers on the network. When the sinkhole domain name was activated the virus was finally able to connect and the virus stopped propagating.

Killer Poke - *Hackerspeak* referring to inducing hardware damage on a machine via insertion of invalid values into a memory-mapped control register; used esp. of various fairly well-known tricks on a computer with limited memory and compute power that can overload and trash analog electronics in the monitor. SOURCE: The Jargon File (version 4.4.7)

Killer Robots - According to the United Nations Convention on Certain Conventional Weapons (CCW), "Killer Robots" can select targets and fire weapons on their own, without human intervention. L.A.W.S. taxonomies can determine accountability and responsibility in various ways.
- **Human-in-the-Loop Weapons** (a robot selects a target and delivers force only with a human command), the human operator determine whether the target selected is a valid enemy combatant. This is essentially what we see today when drones are used to find and attack enemy combatants although the drone does not select the targets.
- **Human-on-the-Loop Weapons** (a robot selects a target and delivers force under the oversight of a human operator who can override the robots' actions), the human operator again is in a position to determine if

the target is a valid enemy combatant. It should be noted that the power to override robots' actions is limited because a robot's decision-making process is measured in nanoseconds.

- **Human-out-of-the-Loop Weapons** (a robot selects a target and delivers force without any human input or interaction), accountability is a tough call because the "Loop" can be very wide indeed. In the final analysis, someone (a person) made a decision to develop the robot, write the rules of engagement, program the robot, weaponize the robot and release the robot into the world.

Command responsibility can be defined as *De jure* (legal) command, and *De facto* (factual) command and can be both military and civilian. Article 28 of the *Rome Statute of the International Criminal Court* states "military commanders are imposed with individual responsibility for crimes committed by forces under their effective command and control if they: either knew or, owing to the circumstances at the time, should have known that the forces were committing or about to commit such crimes. Command responsibility is also referred to as the "*Yamashita standard*" or the "*Medina standard*".

While *The Hague Conventions of 1899* and 1907 do not explicitly create a doctrine of command responsibility, it does uphold a notion that a superior must account for the actions of his subordinates. It also suggests that military superiors have a duty to ensure that their troops act in accordance with international law and if they fail to command them lawfully, their respective states may be held criminally liable. Criminal responsibility would be assigned within military ranks since a commander can be held accountable for an autonomous human subordinate, to hold the commander accountable for killer robots is analogous. See *Lethal Autonomous Weapons Systems*.

Kinect - Kinect is a portmanteau of the words "kinetic" and "connect". Kinect is a line of motion sensing input devices by *Microsoft* for video game consoles and *Windows PCs*. It is a combination of Microsoft-built hardware and software. Based around an RGB camera, depth sensor and multi-array microphone running proprietary software, Kinect combines full-body *3D motion capture, facial recognition* and *voice recognition* capabilities and it enables users to control and interact with their console/computer without the need for a game controller, through a natural user interface using gestures and spoken commands. Kinect is reportedly capable of simultaneously tracking up to six people, including two active players for motion analysis with a feature extraction of 20 joints per player. Efforts are underway to adapt this technology for Kinect-based elderly care and stroke rehabilitation systems. Kinect is being adapted to other "*health aware*" devices for research development. Researchers at the *University of Minnesota* have used Kinect to measure a range of disorder symptoms in children, creating new ways of objective evaluation to detect such conditions as autism, attention-deficit disorder and obsessive-compulsive disorder. Also, see *WiGait*.

Knowledge In, Bullshit Out (KIBO) - A summary of what happens whenever valid data is passed through an organization (or person) that deliberately or accidentally disregards or ignores its significance.

Labeled Faces in the Wild (LFW) - A database of face photographs designed for studying the problem of *unconstrained face recognition*. The data set contains more than 13,000 images of faces collected from the web.

LAN Tap - A *passive Ethernet tap*, requiring no power for operation. To the target network, the LAN Tap looks just like a section of cable, but the wires in the cable extend to the monitoring ports in addition to connecting one target port to the other. The *Throwing Star LAN Tap* (shown below) monitoring ports (J3 and J4) are receive-only; they connect to the receive data lines on the monitoring station, but do not connect to the station's transmit lines. This makes it impossible for the monitoring station to accidentally transmit data packets onto the target network.

LAN Turtle - A covert *Penetration Testing* tool providing *stealth remote access, network intelligence gathering, and man-in-the-middle* surveillance capabilities through a simple graphic shell. A *cracker* can use this to:

- Scan the network using *nmap*
- *DNS Spoof* clients to phishing sites
- *Exfiltrate data* via SSHFS
- Access the entire LAN through a site-to-site *VPN* with the *LAN Turtle* acting as gateway.

Layer 8 - *Hackerspeak* referring to "user" layer on top of the OSI model of computer networking.

Layer of Protection Analysis (LOPA) - A simplified quicker risk assessment approach that provides the much-needed middle ground between a qualitative process hazard analysis and a traditional, expensive quantitative risk analysis. Beginning with an identified accident scenario, *LOPA* uses simplifying rules to evaluate initiating event frequency, independent layers of protection, and consequences to provide an order-of-magnitude estimate of risk. *LOPA* has also proven an excellent approach for determining the safety integrity level necessary for an *instrumented safety system*, an approach endorsed in instrument standards, such as ISA S84 and IEC 61511. According to IEC 61508, the SIL concept (*Safety Integrity Level*) must be related to the dangerous failure rate of *a system*, not just its failure rate or the failure rate of *a component part*, such as the software. Definition of the dangerous failure modes by safety analysis is intrinsic to the proper determination of the failure rate. Hazards of a *control system* must be identified then analyzed through risk analysis. Mitigation of these risks continues until their overall contribution to the hazard are considered acceptable. The tolerable level of these risks is specified as a safety requirement in the form of a target '*probability of a dangerous failure*' in a given period of time, stated as a discrete SIL.

Leapfrog Attack - *Hackerspeak* for use of *userid* and password information obtained illicitly from one host (e.g., downloading a file of account IDs and passwords, tapping *TELNET*, etc.) to compromise another host. Also, the act of TELNETting through one or more hosts in order to confuse a trace (a standard *cracker* procedure). SOURCE: The Jargon File (version 4.4.7)

Least Privilege - The security objective of granting users only those accesses they need to perform their official duties. SOURCE: SP 800-12 Studies have shown that in 2016, 47 percent of analyzed organizations had at least 1,000 sensitive files open to every employee; and 22 percent had 12,000 sensitive files open to every employee.

Leet (1337) - *Hackerspeak, leet* is an alternative alphabet for many languages that is used primarily on the Internet. It uses some characters to replace others in ways that play on the similarity of their glyphs via reflection or other resemblance. For example, *leet* spellings of the word *leet* include 133t and l337. *Leetspeak* is sometimes used to mock *newbies*. The term is derived from the word elite so it is used as an adjective to describe formidable prowess or accomplishment, especially in the fields of online computer hacking and gaming.

Lethal Autonomous Weapons Systems (L.A.W.S.) - Lethal Autonomous Weapons Systems (L.A.W.S.) are *"Killer Robots"* that can select targets and fire weapons on their own, without human intervention. Autonomy is the ability of a system to pursue operational objectives without human intervention. Autonomous weapons are not to be confused with automatic weapons. Automatic weapons, such as machine guns, only fire when a human chooses to fire. Autonomous weapons can function in an open battlefield, under dynamic circumstances and like a human soldier, their behavior may have unintended consequences. Killer Robots are classified according to control and autonomy capability features:

- **Remote Controlled** - Have no autonomy and are operated within a distance via specific frequency bandwidths.
- **Low Level Autonomy** - Perform tasks in an autonomous manner. These may include tracking trajectories, meeting waypoint constraints, carry out scheduled tasks such as photography, perform sensor fusion, visual analysis. Includes ability to plan and execute mission-related tasks.
- **Medium Level Autonomy** - Persists against adverse environmental conditions, including the generation of actions and paths to meet mission objectives while in mission. Advanced abilities involve decision making and re-planning of the tasks under a dynamically changing environment using on-board features. Able to overcome sensor failures.
- **High Level Autonomy** - Has on-board decision-making capability. Instructions are issued at the level of goal statements and the autonomous system should be able to work out a hierarchical plan system based on multi-resolution modeling of the environment under action constraints. Has the ability to interpret a highly-abstract goal and is able to generate sub-goals and sub-plans to achieve higher level goal. Has the ability to re-generate plans in the event of dynamically changing conditions. Interprets high level goals and uses linguistic expressions to its operator for verification purposes.

Existing international law does not explicitly prohibit fully autonomous lethal weapon systems; however, assuming L.A.W.S are not per se illegal, the operational uses must comply with the *law of targeting*. The killing of civilian non-combatants by L.A.W.S. would certainly violate the *Universal Declaration of Human Rights (UDHR)*. While not a treaty itself, the Declaration was explicitly adopted for defining the meaning of the words "fundamental freedoms" and "human rights" in the United Nations Charter (which is binding on all member states). L.A.W.S. using artificial intelligence lacking human control puts non-combatants at significant risk and may not comply with international human rights and humanitarian law. The legality of L.A.W.S. can be summed up by three basic rules:

- The weapon system cannot be indiscriminate by nature.
- The weapon system cannot be "of a nature" to cause "unnecessary suffering or superfluous injury."
- The weapon system can be deemed illegal per se if the harmful effects of the weapon are not capable of being "controlled" (like a biological agent, it cannot be controlled or contained).

L.A.W.S.' full-autonomy poses a grave threat to humanitarian and human rights law. An individual's and a State's responsibility for actions of L.A.W.S. they deploy are fundamental to ensure accountability for violations of international human rights and international humanitarian law. Without the promise of accountability, deterrence and prevention are eliminated – virtually a guarantee of war crimes. Robots have no moral compass and cannot be held responsible if they maim or kill civilians. These are acts that would otherwise require accountability if committed by humans. Simply stated, this is *death by algorithm* and is a violation of a person's right to life, dignity and due process.

Letterbomb - *Hackerspeak* referring to a piece of email containing live data intended to do nefarious things to the recipient's machine. Under *Unix*, a letterbomb can also try to get part of its contents interpreted as a shell command to the mailer. Fortunately, it has been some years since any of the standard Unix/Internet mail software was vulnerable to such an attack (though, as the *Melissa virus* attack demonstrated in early 1999, *Microsoft* systems can have serious problems). SOURCE: The Jargon File (version 4.4.7)

Li-Fi - Wireless data streaming using LED lights to transmit information. LEDs can communicate much faster than Wi-Fi. At 15 gigabits per second, LEDs are more than twice as fast as the fastest Wi-Fi. Li-Fi may be more secure than Wi-Fi because light can't go through walls, hackers would not be able to log on to Li-Fi networks in the same way that they're able to log on to and eavesdrop on Wi-Fi communications.

Link Shortener - See *URL Shortener*.

Live Attack Intelligence - *Norse Corp* provides truly *live attack intelligence* that is able to detect changes in the threat landscape in real-time and fast enough to effectively protect organizations from these types of advanced attacks. This intelligence-based approach to cybersecurity capitalizes on *live threat intelligence* and requires no signatures, so data is never out of date and constantly adapts to the Internet's changing threat landscape. *Live attack intelligence* can be added to:

- **User Authentication Web Page** - This code checks the IP address of a web page visitor before login is allowed to determine the risk/threat factor. An aggregated risk score, geo-location/geo-match, and live risk/threat factor information is returned. Based on this *live attack intelligence*, the connection can then either be blocked/dropped, allowed, or sent for secondary/out of band authentication.

- **The Web Server Level** - A script in the webserver automatically checks the IP address of every incoming connection request to determine the risk/threat factor before they enter the site and can launch an attack. Based on *live attack intelligence*, the connection can then either be blocked/dropped, allowed, or sent to *captcha* or another method of determining whether the visitor is a *bot* versus a human. This method is extremely effective in blocking the most common website attacks such as *SQL injection, binary code injection, cross-site scripting attacks*, as well as unknown and *zero day attacks*.

- **Perimeter Security** - Integrating *live attack intelligence* with common perimeter and edge network devices such as routers, firewalls, load-balancers, and UTM appliances enables protection against a wide breadth of network-based attacks. With *live attack intelligence*, these network layer security appliances and devices can instantly assess the risk level of every incoming and outgoing network connection enabling the blocking malicious traffic before it enters the network and routing higher risk or suspicious traffic for additional analysis or sandboxing by IDS and DPI systems.

- **Website Payment Flow to Detect and Block Fraudulent Transactions** - Integration of *live attack intelligence* into a company's website payment flow helps financial services organizations automate the detection and blocking of fraudulent transactions as they happen and automatically stay current with the latest tactics of fraud perpetrators to reduce risk of attack by *Tor* and *Proxy*-based threats. *Live attack intelligence tools* can instantly accept or deny most orders based on easily defined rules and thresholds.

- **Integrate Live Attack Intelligence with the SIEM System** - Integrating the *SIEM* system with *live attack intelligence* can help identify and remediate unknown and *zero day threats*. A company can correlate external *live attack intelligence* with internal intelligence data to uncover signs of *compromise* and *breach*.

Live Data - *Hackerspeak* for data that is written to be interpreted and takes over program flow when triggered by some un-obvious operation, such as viewing it. One use of such hacks is to break security. For example, some smart terminals have commands that allow one to download strings to program keys; this can be used to write live data that, when listed to the terminal, infects it with a security-breaking virus that is triggered the next time a hapless user strikes that key. In C code, data that includes *pointers to function hooks (executable code)*. SOURCE: The Jargon File (version 4.4.7)

Local Area Network (LAN) - LANs carry messages at relatively high speeds between computers connected by a single communication medium, such as twisted copper wire, coaxial cable or optical fiber. No routing of messages is required within a LAN and the system bandwidth is shared between the computers connected to a small LAN. Larger local networks, such as those that serve a campus or an office building, are composed of many segments interconnected by *switches* or *hubs*. In local area networks, the total system bandwidth is generally high and latency is low.

Location Spoofing – Refers to technique in which the location provided by a smartphone can be spoofed in order to fool a location-based security system. This can be done at the hardware level by directly hacking into the *GPS* hardware or module or simulate it in software and modify it to provide fake location signals to the smartphone operating system; at the OS level by intercepting and modifying the *location APIs* in the smartphone operating system so that they report a fake location to the client application; and at the application level by modifying the client application source code or by intercepting and modifying the final location result that is sent to the location-based server.

Low and Vacuum Pressure Safety Valve (LVPSV) - An automatic system that relieves static pressure on a gas. The pressure is small, negative or positive, and near to atmospheric pressure.

Low Pressure Safety Valve (LPSV) - An automatic system that relieves static pressure on a gas. Used when the difference between the vessel pressure and the ambient atmospheric pressure is small. Spring-operated or weight-loaded.

Lower Explosive Limit (LEL) - The lowest concentration (percentage) of a gas or a vapor in air capable of producing a flash of fire in presence of an ignition source (arc, flame, heat). The term is considered by many safety professionals to be the same as the *lower flammable limit*.

Machine-to-Machine (M2M) - M2 refers to direct communication between devices using any communications channel, including wired and wireless. M2M communication can include industrial instrumentation, enabling a sensor or meter to communicate the data it records (such as temperature, inventory level, etc.) to application software that can use it. Such communication was originally accomplished by having a remote network of machines relay information back to a central hub for analysis, which would then be rerouted into a system like a personal computer. More recent M2M communication has changed into a system of networks that transmits data to personal appliances. The expansion of IP networks has made M2M communication quicker and easier, using less power.

Magic Cookie - *Hackerspeak* for something passed between routines or programs that enables the receiver to perform some operation; a capability ticket or opaque identifier. SOURCE: The Jargon File (version 4.4.7)

Mail Storm - What often happens when a machine with an Internet connection and active users re-connects after extended downtime — a flood of incoming mail that brings the machine to its knees. SOURCE: The Jargon File (version 4.4.7)

Malnet - *Malnets* are large, self-sustaining networks of thousands of compromised servers used to serve malware to PCs users either by tempting them to click on infected links or by drive-by clicks baited through Internet search. First the *malnet* drives a user to the malware. Then the user's computer is infected with a Trojan. Once the computer is compromised it can be used to steal the victim's personal information or money and to lure new users into the *malnet* by using the infected machine to send spam to email contact lists. The top five *malnets* in order of size, are: *Shnakule, Tricki, Rubo, Raskat,* and *Rongdac.* Unlike *botnets* that hardwire a C&C address into the infected machine, *malnets* possess a constantly-shifting command and control system that makes them much harder to shut down; *Shnakule* alone issued changes to its host C&C servers 56,000 times in 2012.

Malware-as-a-Service (MaaS) - MaaS network operates similarly to the software-as-a-service market (e.g. $7,000 a month) that allows criminals to gain access to build-it-yourself malware kits and hosted management services necessary for *cybercrime.* These services include 24/7 customer support hotlines where criminals can have malware tested for detectability and effectiveness around the clock. MaaS also provides access to computer botnets, ("*zombie*" computers that are invisibly infected with malware).

Malware Hunter - A specialized *SHODAN* crawler that explores the Internet looking for command and control (C2s) servers for botnets. It does this by pretending to be an infected client that's reporting back to a C2. The program is constantly scanning for various *Remote Access Trojan* (RAT) programs that are sold illegally on various Internet forums. The list of servers that are serving as the control panels for the Trojan programs is updated in real-time, and security experts use the information to build effective firewalls and security features that would block these programs. It has identified 5,700 RAT servers, most with *Gh0st RAT*.

Mandatory Access Control (MAC) - A type of access control by which the operating system constrains the ability of a subject or initiator to access or generally perform some sort of operation on an object or target. In practice, a subject is usually a process or thread; objects are constructs such as files, directories, TCP/UDP ports, shared memory segments, IO devices, etc. Subjects and objects each have a set of security attributes. Whenever a subject attempts to access an object, an authorization rule enforced by the operating system kernel examines these security attributes and decides whether the access can take place. Any operation by any subject on any object is tested against the set of authorization rules (aka policy) to determine if the operation is allowed.

Mass Flow Controller - A mass *flow controller* (MFC) is a device used to measure and control the flow of liquids and gases. A mass *flow controller* is designed and calibrated to control a specific type of liquid or gas at a particular range of flow rates. The MFC can be given a *setpoint from* 0 to 100% of its full-scale range, but is typically operated in the 10 to 90% of full scale. The device will then control the rate of flow to the given *setpoint*. Mass *flow controllers* require the supply gas or liquid to be within a specific pressure range. *Low pressure* will starve the MFC of fluid and cause it to fail to achieve its *setpoint*. *High pressure* may cause erratic flow rates.

Medical Bar Code Scanning System - Though not strictly a "medical" device, hospitals and healthcare facilities rely heavily on the use of medicine and bloodwork barcode scanning devices to track patient name and identification information (i.e., the barcode values), patient care, prevent medical errors. By tampering with the hospital bar code system, a *cracker* can manipulate the flow of blood samples or medications within the hospital, resulting in the delivery of the wrong medicine types and dosages, as well as mix up blood samples.

Memory Smash - *Hackerspeak* for writing through a pointer that doesn't point to what you think it does. This occasionally reduces your memory to a rubble of bits. Note that this is subtly different from (and more general than) related terms such as a memory leak because it doesn't imply an allocation error or overrun condition. SOURCE: The Jargon File (version 4.4.7)

Metropolitan Area Network (MAN) - This type of network is based on the high bandwidth copper and fiber optic cabling recently installed in some towns and cities for the transmission of video, voice and other data over distances of up to 50 kilometers. A variety of technologies have been used to implement the routing of data in MANs, ranging from *Ethernet* to *ATM*. The *DSL* (Digital Subscriber Line) and cable modem connections now available in many countries are an example. *DSL* typically uses *ATM* switches located in telephone exchanges to route digital data onto twisted pairs of copper wire (using high frequency signaling on the existing wiring used for telephone connections) to the subscriber's home or office at speeds in the range of 1–10 Mbps.

Monitoring and Control Software Override Report - This reports the points overridden by the monitoring and control software, including time overridden and identification of the operator (allegedly) overriding the point.

Message Queueing Telemetry Transport (MQTT) - A machine-to-machine data transfer protocol that is gaining popularity due to its use as a messaging protocol for the *Industrial Internet of Things*. MQTT is designed as a lightweight publish/subscribe messaging transport, used for connections with remote locations where a small code footprint is required and/or network bandwidth is at a premium. It is used for mobile applications because of its small size, low power usage, minimized data packets, publish/subscribe model, bidirectional capabilities and efficient distribution of information to one or multiple receivers. SOURCE: Schneider Electric

Metasploit Project - An *open source* SCADA security project that provides information about vulnerabilities to aid in penetration testing and development of NIDS signatures. Unlike other frameworks, Metasploit can also be used for *anti-forensics*. Expert programmers can write a piece of code exploiting a particular vulnerability, and test it with Metasploit to see if it gets detected. This process can be reversed technically — when a virus attacks using some unknown vulnerability, Metasploit can be used to test the patch for it.

Mining - Users that offer their computing power to verify and record bitcoin transactions (a decentralized digital ledger called a *blockchain*) are called *miners*. This activity is referred to as *mining* and successful miners are rewarded with transaction fees and newly created bitcoins. *Miners* keep the *blockchain* consistent, complete, and unalterable by repeatedly verifying and collecting newly broadcast transactions into a new group of transactions called a *block*. Each *block* contains a cryptographic *hash* of the previous *block*, using the *SHA-256 hashing algorithm* which links it to the previous *block*, thus giving the *blockchain* its name.

Misbug - *Hackerspeak* for an unintended property of a program that turns out to be useful; something that should have been a bug, but turns out to be a feature. SOURCE: The Jargon File (version 4.4.7)

Misfeature - *Hackerspeak* for a feature that eventually causes *lossage*, possibly because it is not adequate for a new situation that has evolved. Since it results from a deliberate and properly implemented feature, a misfeature is not a bug. Nor is it a simple unforeseen side effect; the term implies that the feature in question was carefully planned, but its long-term consequences were not accurately or adequately predicted. SOURCE: The Jargon File (version 4.4.7)

Misnamed Files - A technique used to disguise a file's content by changing the file's name to something innocuous or altering its extension to a different type of file, forcing the examiner to identify the files by file signature versus file extension.

Moby Project - A new *open-source* project to advance the software containerization movement. Moby is designed for system builders, who want to build their own container-based systems, not for application developers. Moby provides a "Lego set" of dozens of components, a framework for assembling them into custom *container-based* systems, and a place for all *container* enthusiasts to experiment and exchange ideas. Think of Moby as the "Lego Club" of *container systems*.

Multiple Levels of Security (MLS) - The application of a computer system to process information with incompatible classifications (i.e., at different security levels), permit access by users with different security clearances and needs-to-know, and prevent users from obtaining access to information for which they lack authorization. There are two contexts for the use of Multilevel Security. One is to refer to a system that is adequate to protect itself from subversion and has robust mechanisms to separate information domains, that is, trustworthy. Another context is to refer to an application of a computer that will require the computer to be strong enough to protect itself from subversion and possess adequate mechanisms to separate information domains, that is, a system we must trust. This distinction is important because systems that need to be trusted are not necessarily trustworthy.

Nested Control Loop - A *nested control loop* is an inner *control loop* within the body of an outer *control loop*. The outer *control loop* establishes the *setpoint* for the inner loop. Then the second pass of the outer *control loop* triggers the inner *control loop* again. An example would be two *nested PID loops*. The integral time might be set to twice (or more) the *loop response time*. In this case, the inner *control loop* must have a faster response time than the outer *control loop*. A break within either the inner or outer *control loop* would *interrupt this process*.

Network Meltdown - *Hackerspeak* refers to a state of complete network overload; the network equivalent of thrashing. This may be induced by a *Chernobyl packet*. Network meltdown is often a result of network designs that are optimized for a steady state of moderate load and don't cope well with the very jagged, bursty usage patterns of the real world. SOURCE: The Jargon File (version 4.4.7)

No Lone Zone - This is an area that must be staffed by two or more qualified individuals. Each individual must be within visual contact with each other and in visual contact with the critical component that requires a no-lone-zone area designation.

noob - *Hackerspeak* for *newbie*, a novice or newcomer, or inexperienced.

Occupancy Sensor/Vacancy Sensor - A lighting control device that detects occupancy of a space by people and turns the lights on or off automatically to save energy, using infrared, ultrasonic or microwave technology. Hack the occupancy sensors and the system can be made to shut off when it should be on and turn on when it should be off.

Office Protected View - *Microsoft Office zero-day* malware allows attackers to silently execute code on targeted machines and secretly install malware if the user has disabled *Protected View*. The exploit executes automatically, making an HTTP request to the attacker's server, from where it downloads an HTML application file, disguised as an *RTF*. Attacks with this *zero-day* start with an adversary emailing a victim a *Microsoft Word* document. The *Word* document contains a booby-trapped *OLE2link object*. While the attack uses *Word* documents, *OLE2link* objects can also be embedded in other Office suite applications, such as *Excel* and *PowerPoint*.

OLE for Process Control (OPC) - *OPC* is a series of standards and specifications for *industrial telecommunication*. *OPC* specifies the communication of real-time plant data between *control devices* from different manufacturers. *OPC* standards define consistent methods of accessing *field data* from *plant floor devices*. This method remains the same regardless of the type and source of data. The *OPC Unified Architecture (UA)* has been specified and is being tested and implemented through an Early Adopters program. It can be implemented with *Java, Microsoft .NET*, or *C*, eliminating the need to use a *Microsoft-Windows-based* platform of earlier *OPC* versions.

OOK (on-off-keying) - A method of exfiltrating data from an *air-gapped* computer that has been infected with malware by sending messages using the LED lights on the front of the case to a variety of cameras and light sensors. For example, 4 kilobytes from the computer's storage can be transmitted covertly by causing the hard drive's LED indicator to blink for less than a fifth of a millisecond.

Open Authorization (OAuth) - OAuth lets apps and services "talk" to each other without logging into your accounts, but without giving them the passwords. OAuth doesn't work through passwords, it works through permission tokens. A vulnerability in OAuth 2.0 could result in an attacker being able to sign into a victim's mobile app account and take control of it. With OAuth exploits, as in the case of the *Google Docs* scam, accounts can be hijacked without the user typing in anything. In the *Google Docs* scheme, the attacker created a fake version of *Google Docs* and asked for permission to read, write and access the victim's emails. By granting the OAuth exploit permission, user effectively gave the bad guys access to their account without needing a password. *Multifactor authentications* do not help in this exploit because passwords are not the entry point. So, when hackers use OAuth exploits, they don't need to enter a password -- the victim duped into giving permission already did. The applications themselves are not required to have a second factor once the user has granted permissions. You need to revoke the permissions to kick out the intruders. If the fake app is shut down the permission would also be automatically revoked.

OpenID Connect (OIDC) - *OICD* is an authentication layer on top of *OAuth 2.0*. *OpenID Connect* allows computing clients to verify the identity of an end-user based on the authentication performed by an authorization server, as well as to obtain basic profile information about the end-user. It uses straightforward *REST/JSON* message flows.

OpenVPN - An *open-source* software application that implements *virtual private network* (VPN) techniques for creating secure *point-to-point* or *site-to-site* connections in routed or bridged configurations and remote access facilities. It is capable of traversing *network address translators* (NATs) and *firewalls*.

Operating-System-Level Virtualization Engines (VEs) - A server software virtualization method in which the kernel of an operating system allows the existence of multiple isolated user-space instances, instead of just one. Also, called *containerization* or *jails* (*FreeBSD jail* or *chroot jail*). It is useful for securely allocating finite hardware resources amongst a large number of mutually-distrusting users. Not as flexible as other *virtualization* approaches since it cannot host a *guest operating system* different from the host one, or a different *guest kernel*.

Owned - *Cracker* slang; often written "0wned". Your condition when your machine has been cracked by a *root exploit*, and the attacker can do anything with it. This sense is occasionally used by *hackers*. SOURCE: The Jargon File (version 4.4.7)

Packet Filtering - *Packet filters*, also called *Network layer firewalls*, operate at a relatively low level of the TCP/IP protocol stack, not allowing packets to pass through the firewall unless they match the established rule set. The firewall administrator may define the rules; or default rules may apply.

Paros - *Java*-based HTTP/HTTPS proxy for testing vulnerability.

Passive Keyless Entry - A *smart key* is an automobile's electronic access and authorization of system that allows the driver to keep the key fob pocketed when unlocking, locking and starting the vehicle. A *smart-key* system can disengage the immobilizer and activate the ignition without inserting a key in the ignition. The system works by having a series of LF (low frequency 125 kHz) transmitting antennas both inside and outside the vehicle. The smart key determines if it is inside or outside the vehicle by measuring the strength of the LF fields. Generally speaking, in order to start the vehicle, the smart key must be inside the vehicle. A "*relay station attack*" is based on the idea of reducing the long physical distance between the car and the regular car owner's smart key fob. By locating a relay station near the car and a second relay station close to the smart key fob, a *cracker* can spoof the signal from a car's wireless key fob 1000 feet away to open a vehicle's doors, and even drive the car away. The cost to build a device like this is about $22. Also, called a *relay hack*.

Patch Cable - A patch cable or patch cord is a cable used to patch in one electronic or optical device to another for signal routing. Devices of different types (switch connected to a computer or a switch to a router) are connected with patch cables. SOURCE: Cablesupply.com

Patch File - In Unix, a patch file (also called a patch for short) is a text file that consists of a list of differences and is produced by running the related diff program with the original and updated file as arguments. Updating files with patch is often referred to as applying the patch or simply patching the files.

Patch Panel - A device or unit featuring a number of jacks, usually of the same or similar type, for the use of connecting and routing circuits for monitoring, interconnecting, and testing circuits in a convenient, flexible manner. Also, called a *patch bay, patch field* or *jack field*.

Patch Velocity - This refers to the rate at which software patches are deployed. A high patch velocity results in higher security than a low patch velocity.

Parallel Test - A test of recovery procedures in which the objective is to parallel an actual business cycle.

Parasitic Wi-Fi - It is possible to induce parasitic signals on the audio front end of voice-command-capable devices such as the *iPhone*. A *cracker* can send radio waves to any *Android or iPhone* that has *Google Now or Siri* enabled. The *hack* uses the phone's headphone cord as an antenna to convert electrical signals that appear to the phone's operating system to be audio coming from the microphone. Anything you can do through the voice interface you can do remotely and discretely through electromagnetic waves.

Pilot Operated Relief Valves (PORV) - A type of *pressure relief valve* (PRV) that uses *system pressure* to seal the valve. PORVs are more complex, resulting in various fail-open failure modes. Also, called *pilot-operated safety valve* (POSV), *pilot-operated pressure relief valve* (POPRV), or *pilot-operated safety relief valve* (POSRV).

Pressure Controller (PC) - A PC is used to maintain a certain pressure in a vessel. For example, an excess of pressure in a gas fuel tank is sent to the fuel gas network or to the flare.

Pressure Relief Valve (PRV) - A *pressure relief valve* is used for emergency relief during overpressure events (e.g., a tank gets too hot and the expanding fluid increases the pressure to dangerous levels). A PRV opens an alternative outlet for the fluids in the system once a set pressure is exceeded, to avoid further build-up of pressure in the protected system. This alternative outlet generally leads to a flare or venting system to safely dispose the excess fluids.

Pwn - A *leetspeak* slang term derived from the verb own, as meaning to appropriate or to conquer to gain ownership. The term implies domination or humiliation of a rival, used primarily in the Internet-based video game culture to taunt an opponent who has just been soundly defeated (e.g., "*You just got pwned!*"). In *script kiddie* jargon, *pwn* means to compromise or control, specifically another computer (server or PC), website, gateway device, or application. It is synonymous with one of the definitions of *hacking* or *cracking*, including *iOS jailbreaking*. The *Pwnie Awards* are awarded by a group of security researchers.

Paywall - Restricting access to Internet content via a paid subscription is called a paywall.

Pebibyte - A multiple of the unit byte for digital information(binary). The prefix pebi (symbol Pi) represents multiplication by 1024^5, therefore: 1 pebibyte = 2^{50} bytes = 1125899906842624 bytes = 1024 tebibytes. Its unit symbol is PiB. The pebibyte is closely related to the petabyte (PB), one pebibyte (1 PiB) is approximately equal to 1.13 PB.

Pen Authentication - Microsoft patent that covers the "system and method for authentication with a computer stylus." This approach authenticates a user by linking a specific stylus to a specific machine with a touch-enabled screen, which would make it a kind of *2FA device* (meaning that the second factor in the *multi-factor authentication* process is based on something you possess) and *gesture recognition* (what and how they draw on the screen).

Perfect Forward Secrecy - When you use an encryption tool like *PGP*, your most sensitive communications are secured by a *private key*. If the key is stolen, a *cracker* could crack all your *future messages* (as well as all past encrypted correspondence). Perfect forward secrecy can be achieved with an encryption system that automatically and frequently changes the *keys* it uses to encrypt and decrypt information, such that if the latest key is compromised, it exposes only a small portion of your sensitive data.

Personal Area Network (PAN) - A computer network used for data transmission amongst devices such as computers, telephones, tablets and personal digital assistants. *PAN*s can be used for communication amongst the personal devices themselves (interpersonal communication), or for connecting to a higher-level network and the *Internet* (an uplink) where one "master" device takes up the role as Internet router.

Phage - A program that modifies other programs or databases in unauthorized ways; esp. one that propagates a *virus* or *Trojan horse*. The analogy, of course, is with phage viruses in biology. SOURCE: The Jargon File (version 4.4.7)

Physical Information Technology (PIT) - *Field devices* in SCADA and building controls systems.

Pointy-Haired Boss (PHB) - *Hackerspeak* based on the Dilbert character, the archetypal half-witted middle-management type. SOURCE: The Jargon File (version 4.4.7)

PowerShell - Task automation and configuration management framework from Microsoft, consisting of a command-line shell and associated scripting language built on the .NET Framework. Can be used as a Fileless Malware cyber-attack.

Prediction Market - *Prediction markets* allow people to "gamble" or "invest" in outcomes of certain events, but they also allow participants to know the probability of a certain event or outcome taking place. This concept is known as the *wisdom of the crowd*, a theory that states that if you ask a large number of people something, their collective answer is often better than the answer given by an expert. *Augur* is a *decentralized prediction market platform* built on the *Ethereum network* that brings together old and new concepts and technologies to create a useful tool.

Priority Interrupt - *Hackerspeak* describes any stimulus compelling enough to yank one right out of hack mode. Classically used to describe being dragged away by a significant other, but may also refer to more mundane interruptions such as a fire alarm going off. Also, called an *NMI* (*non-maskable interrupt*). SOURCE: The Jargon File (version 4.4.7)

Privacy Visor - A bizarre-looking pair of glasses intended to defeat *face detection systems*. The first version worked by blasting camera sensors with beams of near-infrared light, which are invisible to the human eye. A new version uses repeating white patterns printed on a plastic transparency. The dense patterns reflect light back at the camera's sensor, causing enough noise to prevent many algorithms from successfully detecting faces. The problem with this technology is the old paradox of obfuscation: if you're the only one actively trying to hide from surveillance technologies like facial recognition, you're way more likely to stand out. Also, see *CV Dazzle*.

Process Network - The *process network* usually hosts the SCADA servers and human-machine interfaces. The *control network* hosts all the devices that on one side control the actuators and sensors of the physical layer and on the other side provide the control interface to the *process network*.

Proportional–Integral–Derivative Controller (PID controller) - A PID controller is a *control loop feedback mechanism* used in industrial control systems. It continuously calculates the difference between a desired *setpoint* and a measured *process variable* and applies a correction. While proportional control provides stability against small disturbances, it is insufficient for dealing with a steady disturbance.

Protocol Implementation Conformance Statement (PICS) - A document, created by the manufacturer of a device, which describes which potions of the BACnet standard are implemented by a given device.

Provocative Maintenance - *Hackerspeak* for actions performed upon a machine at regularly scheduled intervals to ensure that the system remains in a usable state. So-called because it is all too often performed by a *field technician* who doesn't know what he is doing; such '*maintenance*' often induces problems, or otherwise results in the machine's remaining in an unusable state for an indeterminate amount of time. SOURCE: The Jargon File (version 4.4.7)

Public-Key Encryption - A program on your computer generates a pair of crypto keys. A *private key* or *secret key*, is used for decrypting messages sent to you and does not leave your device. The public key, is used for encrypting messages that are sent to you, and it's designed so that only the corresponding private key can decrypt those messages. The public key can be shared with anyone who wants to encrypt a message to you. Rather than try to break the encryption, a *cracker* may try to impersonate a message recipient in a *man-in-the-middle* attack, hack into your computer and steal the cryptographic key or simply read your decrypted messages.

PunkSPIDER - A global web application vulnerability *search engine*. The driving force behind it is ***PunkSCAN***, a security scanner that can execute a massive number of security scans all at once. Among the types of attacks that *PunkSPIDER* can search for include *Cross-Site Scripting* (XSS), *Blind SQL Injection* (BSQLI), *Operating System Command Injection* (OSCI), and *Path Traversal* (TRAV).

Rabbit Job - *Hackerspeak* for a batch job that does little, if any, real work, but creates one or more copies of itself, breeding like rabbits. SOURCE: The Jargon File (version 4.4.7)

Ralink - An incredibly small USB Wi-Fi adapter.

Ransomware - A type of malware that restricts access to a computer system that it infects in some way, and demands that the user pay a ransom to the operators of the malware to remove the restriction. According to *Symantec*, the U.S was the most targeted country for ransomware and the number of people willing to pay the ransomware was also the highest in the US. Some forms of ransomware systematically encrypt files on the system's hard drive (*cryptoviral extortion*) using a large key that may be technologically infeasible to breach without paying the ransom, while some may simply lock the system and display messages intended to coax the user into paying. Ransomware typically propagates as a *Trojan horse*, whose payload is disguised as a seemingly legitimate file. It should be noted that *cyber-criminals* using the ransomware tactic have yet to figure out a way to let the victim pay for the ransomware using the infected device.

A ransomware attack on a BCS or SCADA would look like this:
The *cracker* exploits a firmware validation bypass vulnerability to replace the legitimate firmware with a malicious one. The *cracker* connects to the targeted device's interface, creates a backup for the configuration of the targeted device, and installs firmware that disrupts regular processes. The victim sees that the compromised device has been disconnected and when they access it for analysis he is greeted with a ransomware message. In order to prevent the victim from restoring the firmware, the *cracker* will disable the firmware and configuration update functionality. The *restore*

factory settings feature does not mitigate the attack in most cases as the process does not restore the original firmware, and this feature can also be disabled by a *cracker*. Recommendation – Don't pay if you can help it. The *cracker* may not restore the system. **Takeaway: Make configuration backups**.

Real-Time Blackhole List (RBL) - *Hackerspeak* refers to a service that allows people to blacklist sites for emitting spam, and makes the blacklist available in real time to electronic-mail transport programs that know how to use RBL so they can filter out mail from those sites. Drastic (and controversial) but effective. SOURCE: The Jargon File (version 4.4.7)

Real Time Streaming Protocol (RTSP, port 554) - RTSP is a network control protocol designed for use in entertainment and communications systems to control streaming media servers. The protocol is used for establishing and controlling media sessions between end points. Clients of media servers issue VCR-style commands, such as play, record and pause, to facilitate real-time control of the media streaming from the server to a client (Video On Demand) or from a client to the server (Voice Recording).

Relief Valve (RV) - An automatic system that is actuated by the static pressure in a liquid-filled vessel. It opens proportionally with increasing pressure. Spring-operated (even spring-loaded).

Relying Party (RP) - A server providing access to a secure software application where a claim is a statement an entity makes about itself in order to establish access. Also, called *relying party applications, claims aware applications* and *claims-based applications*. See *OpenID* and *Open Authorizations*.

Return-to-Libc Cyber-Attack - This is a computer security attack usually starting with a *buffer overflow* in which a subroutine return address on a call stack is replaced by an address of a subroutine that is already present in the process' executable memory, bypassing the NX bit feature (if present) and ridding the attacker of the need to inject their own code. In the *return-to-libc attack* only existing executable code is used. "*ASCII armoring*" is a technique that can be used to obstruct this kind of attack.

Risk Management Framework (RMF) - RMF Risk Management Framework provides a process that integrates security and risk management activities into the system development life cycle. The risk-based approach to security control selection and specification considers effectiveness, efficiency, and constraints due to applicable laws, directives, Executive Orders, policies, standards, or regulations. SOURCE: NIST SP 800-37

Rotary Debugger - *Hackerspeak* refers to a *Pizza*. Considered essential equipment for those late-night or early-morning debugging sessions. SOURCE: The Jargon File (version 4.4.7)

Rubber-Hose Cryptanalysis - *Hackerspeak* for the technique of breaking a code or cipher by finding someone who has the key and applying a rubber hose vigorously and repeatedly to the soles of that luckless person's feet until the key is discovered. Shorthand for any method of coercion: the originator of the term drily noted that it "can take a surprisingly short time and is quite computationally inexpensive" relative to other cryptanalysis methods. SOURCE: The Jargon File (version 4.4.7)

Rubber Ducky - A *Keystroke Injection Attack Platform* hidden in a USB thumb drive. Whether it be a Windows, Mac, Linux or Android device, any *USB* device claiming to be a *Keyboard HID* will be automatically detected and accepted by most modern operating systems. By taking advantage of this inherent trust with *scripted keystrokes* at speeds beyond 1000 words per minute traditional countermeasures can be bypassed.

Rupture Disc - A non-reclosing pressure relief device that, in most uses, protects a pressure vessel, equipment or system from over pressurization or potentially damaging vacuum conditions. A rupture disc is a type of *sacrificial part* because it has a one-time-use membrane that fails at a predetermined differential pressure, either positive or vacuum. The membrane is usually made out of metal, but nearly any material (or different materials in layers) can be used to suit a particular application. Rupture discs provide instant response (within milliseconds) to an increase or decrease in system pressure, but once the disc has ruptured it will not reseal. They can be used as single protection devices or as a backup device for a conventional safety valve; if the pressure increases and the safety valve fails to operate (or can't relieve enough pressure fast enough), the rupture disc will burst. Major advantages of the application of rupture discs compared to using pressure relief valves include leak-tightness and cost. Also, known as a *pressure safety disc, burst disc, bursting disc*, or *burst diaphragm*.

Safety Integrity Level (SIL) - A relative level of risk-reduction provided by a safety function, or to specify a target level of risk reduction. SIL is a measurement of performance required for a safety instrumented function (SIF).

Safety Valve - A safety valve is an automatic system that relieves the static pressure on a gas as a fail-safe in a thermal-hydraulics plant. It usually opens completely, accompanied by a popping sound. An example of a safety valve is a *pressure relief valve* (PRV), which automatically releases a substance from a boiler, pressure vessel, or other system, when the pressure or temperature exceeds preset limits. Pilot-operated relief valves (PORV) are a specialized type of pressure safety valve. The two general types of protection encountered in industry are *thermal protection* and *flow protection*. Spring-operated (even spring-loaded).

Safety Relief Valve (SRV) - An automatic system that relieves by static pressure on both gas and liquid. Spring-operated (even spring-loaded).

Server Message Block (SMB) - This is a network file sharing protocol protocol that relies on lower-level protocols for transport. The transport layer protocol that *Microsoft* SMB protocol is most often used with is *NetBIOS* over *TCP/IP* (NBT). See *SMB Relay Attack.*

Shell Command File (SCF) - This is a file format that supports a very limited set of *Windows Explorer* commands, such as opening a *Windows Explorer* window or showing the Desktop. An SCF is designed to retrieve an icon file from a local hard drive, but malware can redirect the request an SMB server on the Internet (a huge vulnerability).

Spurious Trip Level (STL) - A discrete level for specifying the spurious trip requirements of safety functions to be allocated to safety systems. A safety function should only activate when a dangerous situation occurs. A safety function that activates without the presence of a dangerous situation (e.g., due to an internal failure) causes economic loss. The spurious trip level concept represents the probability that safety function causes a spurious (unscheduled) trip. An STL of 1 means that this safety function has the highest level of spurious trips. The higher the STL level the lower the number of spurious trips caused by the safety system. There is no limit to the number of spurious trip levels. An STL can be specified for a complete safety loop or for individual devices.

Samurai - *Hackerspeak* for a hacker who hires out for legal cracking jobs, snooping for factions in corporate political fights, lawyers pursuing privacy-rights and First Amendment cases, and other parties with legitimate reasons to need an electronic locksmith. SOURCE: The Jargon File (version 4.4.7)

Scanner Hack - Researchers in Israel have shown off a novel technique that would allow attackers to wirelessly command devices using a laser light, bypassing so-called *air gaps*. Firewalls and intrusion detection systems can block communication going to and from suspicious domains and IP addresses over the Internet. To bypass normal detection methods, researchers in Israel were able to use a laser-equipped aerial drone to communicate covertly with malware. The technique uses a *flatbed scanner* as the gateway through which an attacker can send commands to their malware on a victim's network. the attack would also work by hijacking an existing light source installed near the scanner, such as a "smart" lightbulb. The attack could be used against industrial control systems to shut down processes on "air gapped" networks, which aren't directly connected to the Internet.

Scratch - A popular tool to teach children programming. Unlike *Logo*, *Scratch* effectively prepares kids for "real" coding. Also, although Logo is text based and inherently "fussy", children build Scratch projects by dragging and dropping blocks that represent functions, building a program very much like a LEGO structure.

Screen of Death - *Hackerspeak* refers to a special type of error message display onscreen when the system has experienced a fatal error. They typically result in unsaved work being lost and often indicate serious problems with the system's hardware or software. Screens of death are usually the result of a kernel panic, although the terms are frequently used interchangeably. Most screens of death are displayed on an even background color (blue, black, white, yellow) with a message advising the user to restart the computer. The Jargon File (version 4.4.7)

Script Kiddie - *Hackerspeak* for the lowest form of *cracker*; script kiddies do mischief with scripts and rootkits written by others, often without understanding the exploit they are using. Used of people with limited technical expertise using easy-to-operate, pre-configured, and/or automated tools to conduct disruptive activities against networked systems. Since most of these tools are fairly well-known by the security community, the adverse impact of such actions is usually minimal. Also, known as a *skiddie, skid, script bunny, script kitty*, and *skidiot*. SOURCE: The Jargon File (version 4.4.7)

Security Assurance Level (SAL) - A requirements-based approach to selection of security controls using the relative consequences of a successful attack against the control system being evaluated. The consequence analysis identifies the worst, reasonable consequence that could be generated by a specific threat scenario. The SAL provides an overall rating of the criticality based on the users' review of security threat scenarios and estimated consequences which is used to establish the potential for harm and loss both onsite and offsite. The SAL ranges from Low to Very High. **Low**, **Moderate**, and **High** correspond with the levels identified by NIST in the NIST SP800-53 standards, the NIST SP800-60 Volumes 1 and 2 documents, and the CFATS risk-based tiering structure. **Very High** is defined as comprising all controls including all optional enhancements. The *Cyber Security Evaluation Tool* (CSET) developed by the Department of Homeland Defense is used to determine if a facility meets the target SAL set by an agency. CSET also is used to determine the *Mission Assurance Level* (MAC) and the *DoD Assurance Level*.

Security Category (SC) - The characterization of information or an information system based on an assessment of the potential impact that a loss of confidentiality, integrity, or availability of such information or information system would have on organizational operations, organizational assets, or individuals. Establishing an appropriate security category of an information type essentially requires determining the potential impact for each security objective associated with the particular information type. *Federal Information Processing Standards (FIPS 199)* define three levels of *potential* impact on organizations or individuals should there be a breach of security.

- **LOW** − The loss of confidentiality, integrity, or availability could be expected to have a limited adverse effect on organizational operations, organizational assets, or individuals.
- **MODERATE** − The loss of confidentiality, integrity, or availability could be expected to have a serious adverse effect on organizational operations, organizational assets, or individuals.
- **HIGH** − The loss of confidentiality, integrity, or availability could be expected to have a severe or catastrophic adverse effect on organizational operations, organizational assets, or individuals.

EXAMPLE: A power plant contains a SCADA system controlling the distribution of electric power for a large military installation. The SCADA system contains real-time sensor data. The management at the power plant determines that there is no potential impact from a loss of confidentiality, a high potential impact from a loss of integrity, and a high potential impact from a loss of availability of the physical plant equipment. This is written as:

SC sensor data = {(confidentiality, NA), (integrity, HIGH), (availability, HIGH)},

Security Hacker - Someone who seeks to breach defenses and exploit weaknesses in a computer system or network.

Security Key - A specially-designed *thumb drive* you insert into a USB port that uses an individualized secure chip which performs cryptographic functions triggered by a touch of a button on the key. Designed to work with a website that supports the proper protocol such as *Facebook, Google Cloud, Google's Gmail, GitHub and Dropbox. Yubico's* FIDO U2F is a good example.

Security Through Obscurity - *Hackerspeak* referring to most OS vendors' favorite way of coping with security holes — namely, ignoring them, documenting neither any known holes nor the underlying security algorithms, trusting that nobody will find out about them and that people who do find out about them won't exploit them. This *"strategy"* never works for long and occasionally sets the world up for debacles, but once the brief moments of panic created by such events subside, most vendors are all too willing to turn over and go back to sleep. SOURCE: The Jargon File (version 4.4.7)

Security Token Service (STS) - A software-based identity provider responsible for issuing security tokens as part of a claims-based identity system. A client requests access to a secure software application, often called a *relying party*. Instead of the application authenticating the client, the client is redirected to an STS. The STS authenticates the client and issues a *security token*. Finally, the client is redirected back to the *relying party* where it presents the security token. The *token* is the data record in which claims are packed, and is protected from manipulation with strong cryptography. The software application verifies that the *token* originated from an STS trusted by it, and then makes authorization decisions accordingly.

Sentiment Analysis - Social media websites can exploit the moods and insecurities of teenagers by monitoring posts, comments and interactions on the site, Facebook can figure out when people as young as 14 feel "defeated", "overwhelmed", "stressed", "anxious", "nervous", "stupid", "silly", "useless", and a "failure". Such information gathered through a system dubbed *sentiment analysis* could be used by advertisers to target young users when they are potentially more vulnerable. In 2012, Facebook was criticized about the potential of the company to engage in *social engineering* for commercial benefit.

SHODAN - *SHODAN* is a search engine that lets a user find specific types of computers (routers, servers, etc.) connected to the Internet using a variety of filters. This can be information about the server software, what options the service supports, a welcome message or anything else that the client can find out before interacting with the server. *SHODAN* searches the Internet for publicly accessible devices, concentrating on *SCADA* systems. If your building control system is listed on *SHODAN*, it probably can be hacked. *SHODAN* will reveal a device's fingerprint, key exchange (kex) algorithms, server host key algorithms, encryption algorithms, MAC algorithms, and compression algorithms. One of the most popular searches is **"default password."**

Showrooming - The practice of examining merchandise in a traditional brick and mortar retail store or other offline setting, and then buying it online at a lower price. Online stores offer lower prices because they do not have the same overhead cost. The reverse phenomenon of *showrooming* is *webrooming*. In webrooming, customers research a product online and buy in a store.

Sinkhole - A sinkhole is a standard *DNS server* that has been configured to hand out non-routable addresses for all domains in the *sinkhole*, so that every computer that uses it will fail to get access to the real website. Some of the larger botnets have been made unusable by *TLD sinkholes* that span the entire Internet. *DNS Sinkholes* are effective at detecting and blocking malicious traffic, and are used to combat *bots* and other unwanted traffic. Sinkholes can be used both constructively, as has been done for the containment of the *WannaCry* threat, and destructively, for example disrupting *DNS services* in a *DoS* attack. One use is to stop botnets, by interrupting the DNS names the botnet is programmed to use for coordination. The most common use of a hosts file-based sinkhole is to block ad serving sites.

Smart Controls - Communications based on the *Ethernet protocol* making field devices not only self-aware of its status by raising an alarm when a condition occurs that may cause performance to deteriorate, but also system-aware as an autonomous automation asset capable of interacting with others within a network. An example is a variable speed drive motor controlling pumps and actuators. The drive is able to learn a pump operating profile to find an optimized operational point for the pump depending on flow or pressure. SOURCE: Schneider Electric

Smart Rifle Hack - The Linux-powered smart rifle manufactured by *TrackingPoint* is capable of hitting a moving target at a distance of more than a thousand yards. A security vulnerability was discovered that a *cracker* may be able to alter the weapon's aim point; however, he would need to be within 100 feet of the rifle and know the rifle's password.

Smoke Test - *Hackerspeak* refers to a rudimentary form of testing applied to electronic equipment following repair or reconfiguration, in which power is applied and the tester checks for sparks, smoke, or other dramatic signs of fundamental failure. Also, the first run of a piece of software after construction or a critical change.

Sneaker - *Hackerspeak* refers to an individual hired to break into physical places in order to test their security. SOURCE: The Jargon File (version 4.4.7)

SnoopSnitch - This is an app for *Android* devices that analyses your mobile radio traffic to tell if someone is listening in on your phone conversations or tracking your location. Unlike standard antivirus apps, which are designed to combat software intrusions or steal personal info, *SnoopSnitch* picks up on things like fake mobile base stations or *SS7* exploits. *SnoopSnitch* can track *Stingray* or *IMSI catchers*. Currently, *SnoopSnitch* is compatible only with *rooted* Android phones that are equipped with a *Qualcomm* chipset and a stock *Android ROM*.

Software Vulnerabilities - Software vulnerabilities are often exploited by providing unlikely, unusual, or extreme data to a running program. For example, an attacker can exploit a *buffer overflow* vulnerability by providing more input to a program than expected, thereby over-running the area reserved by the program to hold a response. This could corrupt adjacent memory that may hold a *function pointer*. When the program calls through this function it may then jump to an unintended location specified by the attacker. However, in *Windows* programs a potent combination of compile and run-time support from *Control Flow Guard* (CFG) implements control flow integrity that tightly restricts where indirect call instructions can execute.

Spider Food - *Hackerspeak* for keywords embedded (usually invisibly) into a *web page* to attract *search engines* (*spiders*). The intended result of including spider food in one's web page is to ensure that the page appears high on the list of matching entries to a search engine query. SOURCE: The Jargon File (version 4.4.7)

Spoof - As used by *hackers*, refers especially to altering TCP/IP packet source addresses or other packet-header data in order to masquerade as a trusted machine. SOURCE: The Jargon File (version 4.4.7)

Squirrelcide - *Hackerspeak* for what happens when a squirrel shorts out electrical power lines with their furry body. SOURCE: The Jargon File (version 4.4.7)

Startup and Shutdown - Startup and shutdown of a process plant are considered the two most dangerous operational modes of the plant and are limited to the absolute minimum. The best sequence of events is carefully determined considering the chemicals to suit the system and the available hardware. Following is an example of the following steps for of a distillation column startup and shutdown.
   Startup
1. Commissioning
2. Pressure-up
3. Column Heating (and/or cooling)
4. Introduction of feed
5. Introducing heating and cooling sources
6. Bringing column to desired operating conditions
   Shutdown
1. Reducing column rates
2. Shutting down heating and cooling sources
3. Stopping feed
4. Draining liquids
5. Cooling (or heating) the column
6. Bringing the column to atmospheric pressure
7. Eliminating undesirable materials
8. Preparing for opening to atmosphere

Stealth Manager - *Hackerspeak* for a manager that appears out of nowhere, promises undeliverable software to unknown end users, and vanishes before the programming staff realizes what has happened. SOURCE: The Jargon File (version 4.4.7)

Stepping Stone Server - A type of computer security measure implemented in high-security environments consisting of placing several logical security systems in a serial disposition to emulate a physical narrow channel.

Stiction - *Stiction* is the static friction that needs to be overcome to enable relative motion of stationary objects in contact. Any solid objects pressing against each other (but not sliding) will require some threshold of force parallel to the surface of contact in order to overcome static cohesion. *Stiction* is a threshold, not a continuous force. The phenomenon of two such surfaces with areas below the micrometer range come into close proximity and adhering together is also referred to as *stiction*.

Stupids - *Hackerspeak* term used by *samurai* for the *suits* who employ them; succinctly expresses an attitude at least as common, though usually better disguised, among other subcultures of *hackers*. SOURCE: The Jargon File (version 4.4.7)

Suit - *Hackerspeak* for ugly and uncomfortable 'business clothing' often worn by non-hackers. Worn with a 'tie', a strangulation device that partially cuts off the blood supply to the brain. It is thought that this explains much about the behavior of suit-wearers. SOURCE: The Jargon File (version 4.4.7)

Superheated Steam - Steam at a temperature higher than its vaporization (boiling) point at the absolute pressure where the temperature is measured. The steam can cool by some amount, resulting in a lowering of its temperature without condensing from a gas, to a mixture of saturated vapor and liquid. Superheated steam is able to release tremendous quantities of internal energy at the pressures at which reaction turbines and reciprocating piston engines operate. Of prime importance is the fact that water vapor containing entrained liquid droplets is generally incompressible at those pressures. Pressure reduction is <u>required</u> to prevent damage of the internal moving parts. If superheated steam doing work in a reciprocating engine or turbine *cools to a temperature at which liquid droplets form*; the water droplets entrained in the *fluid flow will strike the mechanical parts* with enough force to *bend, crack* or *fracture* them.

Superheater - A device used to convert saturated steam or wet steam into *superheated steam* or *dry steam*. Superheaters are used in steam turbines for *electricity generation, steam engines*, and in processes such as *steam reforming*. There are three types of superheaters: *radiant, convection*, and *separately fired*. A superheater can vary in size from a few tens of feet to several hundred feet. Typically found in a coal-fired thermal power station.

Superloser - *Hackerspeak* for a superuser with no clue — someone with root privileges on a Unix system and no idea what he/she is doing, the moral equivalent of a three-year-old with an unsafetied Uzi. More common than management is aware. SOURCE: The Jargon File (version 4.4.7)

Symmetric Encryption - Symmetric-key algorithms are algorithms for cryptography that use the same cryptographic keys for both *encryption* of plaintext and *decryption* of ciphertext. The keys may be identical or there may be a simple transformation to go between the two keys. The keys, in practice, represent a shared secret between two or more parties that can be used to maintain a private information link. This requirement that both parties have access to the secret key is one of the main drawbacks of symmetric key encryption, in comparison to *public-key encryption* (also known as *asymmetric key encryption*). Symmetric encryption, on its own, is susceptible to attack.

Sysape - *Hackerspeak* derogatory term for a computer operator. SOURCE: The Jargon File (version 4.4.7)

System Mangler - *Hackerspeak* refers specifically to a systems programmer in charge of administration, software maintenance, and updates at some site. Unlike admin, this term emphasizes the technical end of the skills involved. SOURCE: The Jargon File (version 4.4.7)

System Monitoring - There are three generally accepted kinds of valid monitoring output.
- **Alerts** - These require a human must take action right now. Something is happening or about to happen, that some human needs to take action immediately to improve the situation. It is crucial that the human correctly assesses the situation and takes the appropriate corrective action, versus diagnosing incorrectly or taking ineffective steps.
- **Tickets** - A human needs to take action, but not immediately. You have maybe hours, typically, days, but some human action is required.
- **Logging** - No one ever needs to look at this information, but it is available for diagnostic or forensic purposes. The expectation is that no one reads it.

Tape Monkey - *Hackerspeak* refers to a *junior system administrator*, one who might plausibly be assigned to do physical swapping of tapes and subsequent storage. Also, used to dismiss jobs not worthy of a highly-trained sysadmin's ineffable talents. SOURCE: The Jargon File (version 4.4.7)

Tarball - *Tar* is a computer software utility for collecting many files into one archive file, often referred to as a *tarball*, for distribution or backup purposes. The archive data sets created by *tar* contain various file system parameters, such as name, time stamps, ownership, file access permissions, and directory organization.

Tebibyte - A multiple of the unit byte for digital information (binary). The prefix tebi (symbol Ti) represents multiplication by 1024^4, therefore: 1 tebibyte = 2^{40} bytes = 1099511627776 bytes = 1024 gibibytes. Its unit symbol is TiB. The tebibyte is closely related to the terabyte (TB), which is defined as 1012 bytes = 1000000000000 bytes. One tebibyte (1 TiB) is approximately equal to 1.1 TB. In some contexts, the terabyte has been used as a synonym for tebibyte.

TELNET - a network protocol that allows a user on one computer to log onto another computer that is part of the same network.

Ten-Finger Interface - *Hackerspeak* referring to the air gap between two networks that cannot be directly connected for security reasons; interface is achieved by placing two terminals side by side and having an operator read from one and type into the other. SOURCE: The Jargon File (version 4.4.7)

Terabyte - A multiple of the unit byte for digital information. The prefix tera represents the fourth power of 1000, and means 10^{12} in the International System of Units (SI). Approximately one trillion (short scale) bytes 1 TB = 1000000000000 bytes = 1012 bytes = 1000 gigabytes. The unit symbol for the terabyte is TB. A related unit, the tebibyte (TiB), using a binary prefix, is equal to 10244 bytes. One terabyte is about 0.9095 TiB. The terabyte is still also commonly used in some computer operating systems, primarily Microsoft Windows, to denote 1099511627776 (1024^4 or 2^{40}) bytes for disk drive capacity.

Throwaway Account - *Hackerspeak* refers to an inexpensive Internet account purchased on a legitimate ISP for the sole purpose of doing something which requires a valid email address, but being able to ignore spam since the user will not look at the account again. SOURCE: The Jargon File (version 4.4.7)

Three Laws of Robotics - As espoused by Isaac Azimov in 1942.
- A robot may not injure a human being or, through inaction, allow a human being to come to harm;

- A robot must obey the orders given to it by human beings, except where such orders would conflict with the First Law;
- A robot must protect its own existence as long as such protection does not conflict with the First or Second Law.

Tick-List Features - *Hackerspeak* refers to features in software or hardware that customers insist on, but never use. SOURCE: The Jargon File (version 4.4.7)

Tickle a Bug - *Hackerspeak* refers to causing a normally hidden bug to manifest itself through some known series of inputs or operations. SOURCE: The Jargon File (version 4.4.7)

Tinkerbell Program - *Hackerspeak* refers to a monitoring program used to scan incoming network calls and generate alerts when calls are received from particular sites, or when logins are attempted using certain IDs. SOURCE: The Jargon File (version 4.4.7)

Tor (The Onion Router) - Tor is a public *peer-to-peer network*, but unlike other peer-to-peer networks, its main function is anonymization of network traffic. Tor directs Internet traffic through a free, worldwide, volunteer network consisting of more than seven thousand relays to conceal a user's location and usage from anyone conducting network surveillance or traffic analysis. Using Tor makes it more difficult for Internet activity to be traced back to the user: this includes visits to Web sites, online posts, instant messages and other communication forms. Tor was originally developed by the U.S. Naval Research Laboratory for legitimate privacy reasons. Unfortunately, Tor has evolved into a tool used by cybercriminals to control botnets, access online accounts, and use fraudulent financial information to purchase legitimate online goods or services.

Tourist - *Hackerspeak* refers to a guest on the system, especially one who generally logs in over a network from a remote location, email, games, and other trivial purposes. One step below *luser*. SOURCE: The Jargon File (version 4.4.7)

Transient Voltages - Transients are momentary changes in voltage or current that occur over a short period of time. Also, called *surges* or *spikes*. Transients are divided into two categories which are easy to identify: *impulsive* and *oscillatory*. An *impulsive low-frequency transient* rises in 0.1 ms and lasts more than 1 ms. A *medium-*

frequency impulsive transient lasting between 50 ns to 1 ms and *oscillatory transients* between 5 and 500 kHz are less frequent than the *low-frequency types*, but have much *higher amplitude*. These transients may not propagate as easily as the low-frequency types, but *may cause arcing faults* on the power distribution system which result in voltage sag on many power systems. The vast majority of transients are produced within the facility due to *device switching*, *static discharge*, and *arcing*. The inductive "*kick*" from a 5-horsepower motor turning on can produce a transient in excess of 1,000 volts. A motor with a faulty winding, commutator, or other insulation faults can produce a continuous stream of transients exceeding 600 volts! Even transformers can produce a large transient, particularly when energizing. Arcing can generate *transients* from faulty contacts in *breakers, switches*, and *contactors* when voltage jumps the gap. When this gap is "*jumped*" the voltage rises suddenly and the most common effect is an *oscillatory-ring-type transient*. Faulty connections and grounds can produce *arcing*.

Transients cause electronic devices to operate erratically. Equipment could lock up or produced garbled results. These types of disruptions may be difficult to diagnose because faulty transient voltage surge suppression equipment can actually INCREASE the incidents of failure. Integrated circuits may fail immediately. Transients cause motors to run at higher temperatures and interrupt the normal timing of the motor and result in "*micro-jogging*". This type of disruption produces motor vibration, noise, and excessive heat. Transient activity causes early failure of all types of lights. The building's electrical distribution system is also affected by degrading the contacting surfaces of *switches, disconnects,* and *circuit breakers*. Intense transient activity can produce "*nuisance tripping*" of *breakers* by heating the *breaker* and "*fooling*" it into reacting to a non-existent current demand.

Trawl - *Hackerspeak* refers to sifting through large volumes of data (e.g., Usenet postings, FTP archives, or the Jargon File) looking for something of interest. SOURCE: The Jargon File (version 4.4.7)

Trip Valve - A steam engine valve gear developed to improve efficiency. The trip mechanism allows the inlet valve to be closed rapidly, giving a short, sharp cut-off. The valve is opened by the mechanical valve gear mechanism, and when the trip gear trigger releases the mechanism the valve is snapped closed, usually by a spring acting against a *dashpot*. The *trip point* of the valve mechanism, and therefore the *cut-off*, would be adjusted either manually or automatically by the *governor*.

Troglodyte - *Hackerspeak* refers to a hacker who never leaves his cubicle. SOURCE: The Jargon File (version 4.4.7)

True-Hacker - *Hackerspeak* refers to someone who exemplifies the primary values of hacker culture, esp. competence and helpfulness to other hackers. A high compliment. SOURCE: The Jargon File (version 4.4.7)

Trust Anchor - In cryptographic systems with hierarchical structure, a trust anchor is an authoritative entity for which trust is assumed and not derived. In X.509 architecture, a root certificate would be the trust anchor from which the whole chain of trust is derived. The trust anchor must be in the possession of the trusting party beforehand to make any further certificate path validation possible. Most operating systems provide a built-in list of self-signed root certificates to act as trust anchors for applications. The end-user of an operating system or web browser is implicitly trusting in the correct operation of that software, and the software manufacturer in turn is delegating trust for certain cryptographic operations to the certificate authorities responsible for the *root certificates*.

Trusted Platform Module (TPM) - An international standard for a secure cryptoprocessor (hardware), which is a dedicated microcontroller designed to secure hardware by integrating cryptographic keys into devices. Each TPM chip has a unique and secret *RSA key* burned in when it was produced. Using hardware-based security in conjunction with software provides more protection than a software-only solution.

Typosquatting - This is the practice of occupying web domain names that are misspellings of popular domains. Also, see *cyber-squatting*.

Ubertooth One - An *open source Bluetooth* test tool from Michael Ossmann. An affordable platform that can be used for Bluetooth monitoring and for the development of new Bluetooth and wireless technologies.

Universal Description, Discovery and Integration (UDDI) - UDDI is an XML-based standard for describing, publishing, and finding Web services. UDDI is a specification for a distributed registry of Web services. UDDI is platform independent, open framework and it can communicate via SOAP, CORBA, Java RMI Protocol. UDDI is an open industry initiative enabling businesses to discover each other and define how they interact over the Internet.

Ubuntu - A *Debian-based Linux operating system* for personal computers, tablets and smartphones, where *Ubuntu Touch* edition is used; and also runs network servers, usually with the *Ubuntu Server* edition, either on physical or virtual servers (such as on mainframes) or with containers, that is with enterprise-class features; runs on the most popular architectures, including server-class *ARM-based*.

Underfloor Air Distribution (UFAD) - An air distribution strategy for providing ventilation and space conditioning in buildings as part of the design of an HVAC system. UFAD systems use an underfloor supply plenum located between the structural concrete slab and a raised floor system to supply conditioned air through floor diffusers directly into the occupied zone of the building.

Underground Cable Locator - This device is used to detect buried power cables, CATV cables, gas and water pipes, sewer lines, telephone cables, fiber optic cables with sheath. They generally consist of a transmitter and a receiver. The transmitter puts an electrical signal onto the cable or pipe being traced, while the receiver picks up that signal, allowing the operator to trace the signal's path and follow the cable being located. The electromagnetic field created can usually be set to a specific frequency, depending on the type of conductor in the cable. Lower frequencies bleed over less and detect the conductor better. An *underground cable* is typically buried 4 or 5 feet and there may be other services a lot closer to the surface. *Premises wiring* is located on the other side of sheet rock and the locator is about 6 inches from the cable.

Uniform Resource Locator (URL) - A web address, is a reference to a web resource that specifies its location on a computer network and a mechanism for retrieving it. Thus http://www.example.com is a URL. URLs occur most commonly to reference web pages (http), but are also used for *file transfer (ftp), email* (mailto), *database access* (JDBC), and many other applications.

Uninteresting - *Hackerspeak* referring to a problem that, although nontrivial, can be solved simply by throwing sufficient resources at it. Hackers regard uninteresting problems as intolerable wastes of time, to be solved (if at all) by lesser mortals. SOURCE: The Jargon File (version 4.4.7)

Unix Weenie - *Hackerspeak* refers to a derogatory play on '*Unix wizard*', common among hackers who use Unix by necessity but would prefer alternatives. The implication is that although the person in question may consider mastery of Unix arcana to be a wizardly skill, the only real skill involved is the ability to tolerate (and the bad taste to wallow in) the incoherence and needless complexity that is alleged to infest many Unix programs. SOURCE: The Jargon File (version 4.4.7)

Upper Explosive Limit (UEL) - Highest concentration (percentage) of a gas or a vapor in air capable of producing a flash of fire in presence of an ignition source (arc, flame, heat). Concentrations higher than UEL are "too rich" to burn.

URL Shortener - URL Shortener is used to create shorter aliases for long URLs (Uniform Resource Locator). Users are redirected to the original URL when they hit these aliases. When someone visits the *Short Link*, it is automatically *redirected* to the Destination URL. URL Shortening is used by companies for branding and to track them by counting the clicks on the link. Unfortunately, short links have been used on *phishing emails* designed to look like *Gmail* alerts containing a short link that led to a fake webpage to harvest the victim's password. Some used *Google's* own style and look for a security alert. To a distracted or untrained eye, there would be no difference between this and the real thing. Also, called a *Link Shortener*.

Vacuum Pressure Safety Valve (VPSV) - An automatic system that relieves static pressure on a gas. Used when the pressure difference between the vessel pressure and the ambient pressure is small, negative and near to atmospheric pressure. Spring-operated or weight-loaded.

Vadding - *Hackerspeak* referring to a leisure-time activity of certain hackers involving the covert exploration of the 'secret' parts of large buildings — basements, roofs, freight elevators, maintenance crawlways, steam tunnels, and the like. A few go so far as to learn *locksmithing* in order to synthesize vadding keys. This term dates from the late 1970s, before which such activity was simply called 'hacking'; the older usage is still prevalent at MIT.

Valve - An in-line device in a fluid-flow system that can interrupt flow, regulate the rate of flow, or divert flow to another branch of the system. There are many different types and styles of valves, but all primarily serve the common purpose of balancing a system. Valve types include:

1. **Three-way valves**. Most associated with constant volume systems, these devices are used to modulate water flow to the load without changing the constant volume of water flow to the system.

2. **Two-way valves**. Most associated with variable speed/variable volume systems, these devices modulate flow to the load by changing the constant volume of water flow to the system.

3. **Manual balancing valves**. These have an adjustable orifice that can be changed by hand to provide a specific pressure drop and flow.

4. **Flow-limiting valves**. These valves vary the flow based on differential pressure to provide a specific flow rate.

Venus Flytrap - *Hackerspeak* referring to a dedicated gateway machine with special security precautions on it, used to service outside network connections and dial-in lines. The idea is to protect a cluster of more loosely administered machines hidden behind it from *cracker*s. The typical firewall is an inexpensive micro-based Unix box kept clean of critical data, with a bunch of modems and public network ports on it but just one carefully watched connection back to the rest of the cluster. The special precautions may include threat monitoring, callback, and even a complete iron box keyable to particular incoming IDs or activity patterns. SOURCE: The Jargon File (version 4.4.7)

Vibrational Energy Harvester (VEH) A small piezoelectric device using micro-electro-mechanical systems technology that is capable of harvesting microwatts of electricity from background vibrations to power miniature devices like *sensor nodes*. For example: a VEH was attached to a wireless temperature sensor and subjected to vibrations of 353 Hz at 0.64g. The system generated enough power to take environmental readings and send data to a base station at 15 second intervals.

VID/PID Numbers - A *USB* device that is plugged in identifies itself by its *VID/PID* combination. A VID is a 16-bit vendor number (Vendor ID). A PID is a 16-bit product number (Product ID). The PC uses the VID/PID combination to find the drivers (if any) that are to be used for the USB device. For this to work, the VID/PID combination must be unique, in the sense that each USB device with the same VID/PID will use the same driver. A *cracker* can change the VID/PID on a thumb drive to fool the computer into thinking it is another device, with the intent to load *malicious payload*, either a file or *scripted code*.

Video Toaster - *Hackerspeak* refers to any computer system designed specifically for video production and manipulation. SOURCE: The Jargon File (version 4.4.7)

Virtual Beer - *Hackerspeak* for praise or thanks. Used universally in the *Linux* community. SOURCE: The Jargon File (version 4.4.7)

Virtual Friday - *Hackerspeak* refers to the last day before an extended weekend, if that day is not a 'real' Friday. Also, called *Logical Friday*. The next day is often also a holiday or taken as an extra day off, in which case Wednesday of that week is a virtual Friday (and Thursday is a virtual Saturday, as is Friday). There are also virtual Mondays that are actually Tuesdays, after the three-day weekends associated with many national holidays. SOURCE: The Jargon File (version 4.4.7)

Virtuous Circle and Vicious Circle - A complex chains of events which reinforce themselves through a feedback loop. A virtuous circle has favorable results, while a vicious circle has detrimental results.

VirusTotal - A *malware aggregation platform* created by *Google*. *VirusTotal* is a free *website* that analyzes suspicious files (up to 128 MB) and URLs and facilitates the quick detection of viruses, worms, trojans, and all kinds of malware. It is used to check for viruses that the user's own antivirus may have missed, or to verify against any false positives.

Voice-Net - *Hackish* way of referring to the telephone system, analogizing it to a digital network. SOURCE: The Jargon File (version 4.4.7)

Voodoo Programming - *Hackerspeak* referring to the use by guess or cookbook of an obscure or hairy system, feature, or algorithm that one does not truly understand. The implication is that the technique may not work, and if it doesn't, one will never know why. Almost synonymous with *black magic*, except that *black magic* typically isn't documented and nobody understands it. Also, things programmers do that they know shouldn't work, but they try anyway, and which sometimes actually work, such as recompiling everything. SOURCE: The Jargon File (version 4.4.7)

Vulnerability - A weakness in an information system or component (e.g., security procedures, hardware design, and internal controls) that could be exploited, attacked or fail. Vulnerabilities include susceptibility to physical dangers, such as fire or water, unauthorized access to sensitive data, entry of erroneous data, denial of timely service, fraud, etc.

Vulture Capitalist - Pejorative *hackerism* for *'venture capitalist'*, deriving from the common practice of pushing contracts that deprive inventors of control over their own innovations and most of the money they ought to have made from them. SOURCE: The Jargon File (version 4.4.7)

Wabbit - *Hackerspeak* referring to any hack that includes infinite self-replication, but is not a *virus* or *worm*. SOURCE: The Jargon File (version 4.4.7)

Wall Follower - *Hackerspeak* referring to a person or algorithm that compensates for lack of sophistication or native stupidity by efficiently following some simple procedure shown to have been effective in the past. Used of an algorithm, this is not necessarily pejorative; it recalls *'Harvey Wallbanger'*, the winning robot in an early AI contest. Harvey successfully solved mazes by keeping a 'finger' on one wall and running till it came out the other end. This was inelegant, but it was mathematically guaranteed to work on simply-connected mazes — and, in fact, *Harvey* outperformed more sophisticated robots that tried to 'learn' each maze by building an internal representation of it. Used of humans, the term is pejorative and implies an uncreative, bureaucratic, by-the-book mentality. SOURCE: The Jargon File (version 4.4.7)

Wide Area Network (WAN) - WANs carry messages at lower speeds between nodes that are often in different organizations and may be separated by large distances. They may be located in different cities, countries or continents. The communication medium is a set of communication circuits linking a set of dedicated computers called *routers*. They manage the communication network and route messages or *packets* to their destinations. In most networks, the routing operations introduce a delay at each point in the route, so the total latency for the transmission of a message depends on the route that it follows and the traffic loads in the various network segments that it traverses.

Wannabee - *Hackerspeak* refers to a would-be hacker. When used of any professional programmer, CS academic, writer, or suit, it is derogatory, implying that said person is trying to cuddle up to the hacker mystique but doesn't, fundamentally, have a prayer of understanding what it is all about. SOURCE: The Jargon File (version 4.4.7)

Warez - *Crackerspeak* meaning a cracked version of commercial software, that is versions from which copy-protection has been stripped. Hackers recognize this term, but don't use it themselves. SOURCE: The Jargon File (version 4.4.7)

Washing Software - The process of recompiling a software distribution (used more often when the recompilation is occurring from scratch) to pick up and merge together all of the various changes that have been made to the source. SOURCE: The Jargon File (version 4.4.7)

Wave a Dead Chicken - *Hackerspeak* refers to performing a ritual in the direction of crashed software or hardware that one believes to be futile, but is nevertheless necessary so that *suits* are satisfied that an appropriate degree of effort has been expended. SOURCE: The Jargon File (version 4.4.7)

Webrooming - The practice of researching a product online and buy in a brick and mortar retail store. The reverse phenomenon is showrooming – examining merchandise in a traditional brick and mortar retail store or other offline setting, and then buying it online at a lower price.

Web Ring - Two or more web sites connected by prominent links between sites sharing a common interest or theme. Usually such cliques have the topology of a ring, in order to make it easy for visitors to navigate through all of them.

Web Services Description Language (WSDL) - WSDL is an XML-based language for describing Web services and how to access them. WSDL is the standard format for describing a web service, how to access it and what operations it will perform.

Web Toaster - A small specialized computer, shipped with no monitor or keyboard or any other external peripherals, pre-configured to be controlled through an *Ethernet* port and function as a WWW server. Products of this kind (for example the *Cobalt Qube*) are often about the size of a toaster. SOURCE: The Jargon File (version 4.4.7)

Website Reputation Service - Maintains a blacklist of known bad websites.

Wedgie - *Hackerspeak* refers to a *bug*. SOURCE: The Jargon File (version 4.4.7)

Wetware - A term used to describe the elements equivalent to hardware and software found in a person, namely the central nervous system and the human mind. The prefix "wet" is a reference to the water found in living creatures. Also, called *meatware, jellyware, Liveware* as in a "Liveware Problem", and *biological interface error*.

Whack - According to *arch-hacker* James Gosling (designer of *NeWS*, *GOSMACS* and *Java*), to "...modify a program with no idea whatsoever how it works." It is actually possible to do this in nontrivial circumstances if the change is small and well-defined and you are very good at *glarking* things from context. SOURCE: The Jargon File (version 4.4.7)

Whacker - *Hackerspeak* referring to a person, similar to a *hacker*, who enjoys exploring the details of programmable systems and how to stretch their capabilities. Whereas a *hacker* tends to produce great hacks, a whacker only ends up whacking the system or program in question. *Whackers* are often quite egotistical and eager to claim wizard status, regardless of the views of their peers. SOURCE: The Jargon File (version 4.4.7)

Wheel Wars - *Hackerspeak* referring to when student hackers hassle each other by attempting to log each other out of the system, delete each other's files, and otherwise wreak havoc, usually at the expense of the lesser users. SOURCE: The Jargon File (version 4.4.7)

Wheel of Misfortune - A statistically adjusted disaster exercise selection mechanism for picking a possible operations breakdown scenario or equipment failure, followed by role playing, in which one person plays the part of the "system" -- and the other person plays the part of the on-call engineer.

Wireless Device - A device that can connect to a manufacturer's system via radio or infrared waves to typically collect/monitor data, but also in cases to modify control *setpoint*s. Something to be removed or disabled immediately if you have any sense at all.

Wireless Fidelity (Wi-Fi) - Any type of 802.11 network.

Wireless Interface Module - Provides a common interface to wireless sensors and switches. These should be extremely rare because they are not secure and are easily compromised by any garden-variety *cracker*, junior-grade.

Wi-Fi Pineapple - An advanced wireless device used for *penetration testing* or used by *crackers* as a *rogue access point* for *reconnaissance*, *man-in-the-middle*, *tracking*, *logging* and *reporting*.

Wi-Fi Spy - As a Wi-Fi router communicates with other devices, the router is also gathering information about how its signals are traveling through the air, and whether they're being disrupted by obstacles or interference. With that data, the router can make small adjustments to communicate more reliably with the devices it's connected to. Wi-Fi routers can use this capability to monitor humans in detailed ways. As people move through a space their bodies affect the Wi-Fi signal, absorbing some waves and reflecting others. By analyzing the exact ways that a Wi-Fi signal is altered when a person moves through a space, researchers have been able to identify a particular person either based on their body shape or the specific way they walk; they can "see" what someone writes with their finger in the air; and even read a person's lips with startling accuracy even if a router isn't in the same room. Researchers in China posted scientific research, detailing a system that can accurately identify humans as they walk through a door nine times out of ten. Another system called "WiKey" could tell what keys a user was pressing on a keyboard by monitoring minute finger movements. Once trained, WiKey could recognize a sentence as it was typed with 93.5 percent accuracy—all using nothing but a commercially available router and some custom software. Researchers have also presented Wi-Fi technology that could "hear" what people were saying by analyzing the distortions and reflections in Wi-Fi signals created by their moving mouths. SOURCE: The Atlantic Aug 24, 2016

WiGait - A *"health-aware"* device for the home that uses radio waves with 1/1000th the power of a wi-fi signal, to track a person's movements *Gait velocity*. The simple measurement of how fast you walk, coupled with your stride length, gives doctors a tangible measure of elderly mobility, along with complications stemming from diseases like Parkinson's and Alzheimer's. Unlike the *Kinect*-based elderly care and stroke rehabilitation systems which uses a webcam, *WiGait* does not use an image and just tracks the movements, even through walls.

Windows Management Instrumentation (WMI) - Task automation and configuration management framework from *Microsoft*. WMI has access to every resource on the computer and can perform various tasks such as execute files, delete and copy files, or change registry values. WMI can be used as a *Fileless Malware* cyber-attack by using inherent "features" built into Windows to turn the operating system against itself to compromise a computer network.

Wire Ladder - A wire ladder is a clean way to organize cables in a data center or server room. They are designed to hold Cat5, Cat6, Cat7, fiber optic, or coaxial cable and can be suspended from the ceiling, attached vertically to a wall, or installed below the raised floor. Also, called a *cable raceway, cable runway, cable tray, cable basket tray, wire mesh cable tray, cable organizer*, or *cable ladder*. SOURCE: Cablesupply.com

Wirehead - *Hackerspeak* refers to a hardware hacker, especially one who concentrates on communications hardware. Also, an expert in local-area networks. A wirehead can be a network software wizard too, but will always have the ability to deal with network hardware, down to the smallest component. Wireheads are known for their ability to lash up an *Ethernet* terminator from spare resistors, for example. SOURCE: The Jargon File (version 4.4.7)

Wireless Local Area Network (WLAN) - WLANs are designed for use in place of wired LANs to provide connectivity for mobile devices, or simply to remove the need for a wired infrastructure to connect computers within homes and office buildings to each other and the Internet. They are in widespread use in several variants of the IEEE 802.11 standard (*Wi-Fi*), offering bandwidths of 10–100 Mbps over ranges up to 1.5 kilometers.

Wireless Personal Area Network (WPAN) - A personal area network—a network for interconnecting devices centered on an individual person's workspace—in which the connections are wireless. Wireless PAN is based on the standard *IEEE 802.15*. There are several kinds of wireless technologies used including *Bluetooth, Infrared Data Association* and *ZigBee*. A *Bluetooth PAN* is also called a piconet and is composed of up to 8 active devices. *ZigBee* is a wireless low-power standard that connects embedded technologies in personal area networks such as "smart" lightbulbs. A key concept in WPAN technology is known as "*plugging in*". In the ideal scenario, when any two WPAN-equipped devices come into close proximity (within several meters of each other) or within a few kilometers of a central server, they can communicate as if connected by a cable. Another important feature is the ability of each device to lock out other devices selectively, preventing needless interference or unauthorized access to information.

w00t - *Hackerspeak* similar to "Yay!", as in: "w00t!!! I just got a raise!" Some claim this is a bastardization of "root", the highest level of access to a system, and said as an exclamation upon gaining root access. SOURCE: The Jargon File (version 4.4.7)

YARA - A computer forensics tool that lets researchers sift through a lot of files and networks using a search string to search for specific files.

YARD Stick (Yet Another Radio Dongle) - A USB device that can transmit or receive digital wireless signals at frequencies below 1 GHz.

YouTube Faces (YTF) - *Facial recognition* software that is modeled similar to the *LFW*, but focuses on video clips. The YTF dataset of *face videos* is designed for studying the problem of unconstrained face recognition in videos. Face recognition in video is becoming increasingly important due to the abundance of video data captured by surveillance cameras, mobile devices, Internet uploads, and other sources. The data set contains 3,425 videos of 1,595 different people.

Yow! - *Hackerspeak* expression of humorous surprise or emphasis. SOURCE: The Jargon File (version 4.4.7)

Yoyo Mode - *Hackerspeak* refers to the state in which the system is said to be when it rapidly alternates several times between being up and being down. SOURCE: The Jargon File (version 4.4.7)

Zbeba - *Hackerspeak* for a 'moron'. Used to describe *newbies* who are behaving with *especial cluelessness*. SOURCE: The Jargon File (version 4.4.7)

Zebibyte - A multiple of the unit byte for digital information (binary). The prefix zebi (symbol Zi) represents multiplication by 1024^7, therefore: 1 zebibyte = 2^{70} bytes = 1180591620717411303424 bytes = 1024 exbibytes. Its unit symbol is ZiB.

Zed Attack Proxy (ZAP) - An *open-source* web application *security scanner* intended to be used by both those new to application security as well as professional penetration testers. When used as a *proxy server* it allows the user to manipulate all of the traffic that passes through it, including traffic using https.

ZigBee Light Link (ZLL) - A low-power *mesh network* standard used by connected lighting systems. The ZLL standard is insecure by design. The security mechanisms of ZLL-based connected lighting systems contain fallback solutions and flaws that allow an attacker to remotely control the lights from a distance. Researchers were also able to extend the intended wireless range of maximum 2 meters for configuring a ZLL device, to over 30 meters, thus making ZLL-based systems susceptible to war driving.

Zipperhead - *Hackerspeak* for a person with a closed mind. SOURCE: The Jargon File (version 4.4.7)

Zombie - *Hackerspeak* refers to a machine, especially someone's home box, that has been cracked and is being used as part of a second-stage attack by miscreants trying to mask their home IP address. Especially used of machines being exploited in large gangs for a mechanized *denial-of-service attack*; the image that goes with this is of a veritable army of zombies mindlessly doing the bidding of a necromancer. SOURCE: The Jargon File (version 4.4.7)

ZoomEye - ZoomEye is a Chinese search engine similar to *SHODAN* that allows the user find specific network components. ZoomEye is *hacker-friendly* and uses *Xmap* and *Wmap* at its core for grabbing data from publicly exposed devices and web services (http://ics.zoomeye.org). ZoomEye allows you to search by:

- **Application name and version** number
- **Location**: **country** code (for example: UK, IT, ES, FR, CN, JP.) and name of **city**
- **Port** number
- **Name of the operating system** (for example os:linux)
- **Service name**
- **Hostname** (for example hostname:google.com)
- **IP address** (for example ip:8.8.8.8)
- **CIDR segment** (for example cidr:8.8.8.8/24)
- **Domain name** (for example site:google.com)
- **Headers** in HTTP request
- **SEO keywords** defined inside <meta name="Keywords">
- **Description** inside <meta name="description">
- **Title** inside <title>
- **Apache httpd** – finds results for Apache http servers
- **device:"webcam"** – finds a list of webcams with an Internet connection

One of the most popular searches is "***default password***."

CYBER-ATTACKS

Not all these cyber-attacks are direct attacks on a BCS. Some are merely a way to get into a network so a cyber-physical attack can be carried out.

../ (dot dot slash) Cyber-Attack - Also called a *directory traversal,* the attack consists of exploiting insufficient security validation / sanitization of user-supplied input file names, so that characters representing "traverse to parent directory" are passed through to the file *APIs*. The goal is to use an affected application to gain unauthorized access to the file system. This attack exploits a lack of security (the software is acting exactly as it is supposed to) as opposed to exploiting a *bug* in the code. Also, known as the *path traversal*, *directory climbing*, and *backtracking*. Some forms of this attack are also *canonicalization attacks*.

Account Harvesting Attack - Account Harvesting is the process of collecting all the legitimate account names on a system. Although, not specifically a cyber-physical attack, it is one of the first steps.

Account Takeover Attack - Banks often employ two-step security measures as an added layer of protection against password theft and fraud. But several *Man in the Browser* (MitB) style attacks have recently been shown to be able to defeat even two-factor authentication systems. Using this method, a cybercriminal constructs a fake bank website and entices the user to that website (sometimes *spearfishing*). The user then inputs their credentials and the cybercriminal in turn uses the credentials to access the bank's real website. When executed properly, the victim never realizes they are not actually at the legitimate bank's website. These can be very sophisticated and complicated to execute which is reflective of the fact that they are created by motivated, coordinated, and well-funded organized cyber-crime syndicates. In many cases, the malware must be custom-made for each bank website, which involves extensive coding on the part of the *malware* authors. Destination accounts must also be created at the targeted bank so that the cybercriminal has a place to deposit the stolen money. Access to the stolen funds is achieved by a network of *money mules*, which must be recruited to access the destination accounts and move the money out of the bank.

ACK Piggybacking Attack - When a *cracker* sends an ACK inside another packet to the same destination.

Active Attack - An actual assault perpetrated by an intentional threat source that attempts to alter a system, its resources, its data, or its operations.

Active Content - Electronic documents that can carry out or trigger actions automatically on a computer platform without the intervention of a user. Software in various forms that is able to automatically carry out or trigger actions on a computer platform without the intervention of a user. SOURCE: SP 800-28, CNSSI-4009

Active Cyber-Physical Attack - An intentional cyber-attack perpetrated that attempts to alter a SCADA system, its resources, its data, or its operations.

Active Medical Devices (AMD) - An active medical device is one that interfaces directly with a patient to *administer medical treatment.* Some examples of AMDs are: *X-Ray machine, MRI, CT Scanner, Pet Scanner, infusion pumps, surgical lasers, medical ventilators, extracorporeal membrane oxygenation machines* and *dialysis machines.* Many active medical devices today include a computer to control the machine and communicate with the hospital network, so it is possible for them to be hacked. See my book *"Cybersecurity for Hospitals and Healthcare Facilities"* for more information.

Active Patient Monitoring Device Cyber-Physical Attack - These are networked in-hospital patient monitoring devices that require a timely response (e.g. a monitor that is intended to detect life-threatening *arrhythmias* such as *ventricular fibrillation* or a device used to actively monitor *diabetes* for time-sensitive intervention). These devices can be hacked. See my book *"Cybersecurity for Hospitals and Healthcare Facilities"* for more information.

Address Space Probe Attack - An intrusion technique that attempts to map IP address space as the information gathering prelude to an attack. The *cracker* is looking for security holes that might be exploited to compromise system security.

Advanced Persistent Threats (APT) - A network attack in which an unauthorized person gains access to a network and stays there undetected for a long period of time. The intent is to steal data rather than to cause damage to the network or organization. A persistent presence is sometimes called *"consolidation"*. *APT*s can wait a long time before becoming active. By performing a *gap analysis* of the network configuration, hidden *APT*s can be made to show themselves, either by detection methods or making them become visible by exposing themselves through their designed behavior.

Alarm Flooding Attack - Alarm Flooding (annunciation of more alarms in a given period of time than a human operator can respond) to confuse building maintenance personnel. Ten alarms per minute is typically the most alarms a technician can handle.

Amplification Attack - A type of DDoS attack, when a single UDP packet generates tens or hundreds of times the bandwidth in its response in a reflected *DoS* attack.

Android Network Scan Attack - Researchers have discovered hundreds of vulnerable *apps* which allow *crackers* to inject them with malicious code which, upon downloading, steal all data from an infected *Android* device. These *apps* create open ports on *smartphones* leaving open doors for any malicious code. Only fix is to uninstall the app.

Annoyware - *Hackerspeak* for a type of shareware that frequently disrupts normal program operation to display requests for payment to the author in return for the ability to disable the request messages. Also, called *nagware*. See also *careware, charityware, crippleware, freeware, guiltware, postcardware.* SOURCE: The Jargon File (version 4.4.7)

App Permissions - *Android* applications use *app* permissions defined before the *app* is allowed to do certain things like access the Internet for example. This stops *apps* from doing whatever they want without the user's knowledge. Some app permissions include: ways to purchase content inside the *app* itself (such as in-game currency); read sensitive log data, read web bookmarks and history, retrieve *apps* and retrieve system internal state (this can reveal very sensitive information about the device); control the device's mobile *network settings* and possibly intercept the data received; find accounts on the device, see and modify the owner's contact card and add or remove contacts; access the user's calendar and events; get the device's location from the network and the device's *GPS*; directly call phone numbers without the user knowing; *mount and unmount* external *storage* as well as format external storage; take pictures and video; use the device's microphone to record audio without the user's permission; and many others. *App* permissions generally don't have the ability to change your password. I highly recommend you <u>revoke</u> as many permissions as you can and recheck every few months.

Applet Attack - An application program that uses the client's web browser to provide a user interface and disable the *Java* security *sandbox*.

Appliance Cyber-Physical Attack - With the growth of the *Internet of Things*, even common appliances such as dishwashers, coffee makers, clothes dryers and baby nursery room monitors connect to the Internet and could be used to gather intelligence. Manufacturers use this capability to troubleshoot performance of their equipment, monitor usage and improve the customer "experience". Unfortunately, knowing when you use the appliance provides data could help *crackers geo-locate* your current position, and learn your habits and schedule.

ARP Spoofing Attack - A technique by which an attacker sends (*spoofed*) *Address Resolution Protocol* (ARP) messages onto a local area network. Generally, the aim is to associate the attacker's *MAC address* with the *IP address* of another host, such as the default gateway, causing any traffic meant for that IP address to be sent to the attacker instead. *ARP spoofing* may allow an attacker to intercept data frames on a network, *modify* the traffic, *or stop* all traffic. Often the attack is used as an opening for other attacks, such as *denial of service, man in the middle*, or *session hijacking* attacks. Also, called *ARP cache poisoning*, or *ARP poison routing*.

Attack Vectors - Ways in which your *BCS* or *CMMS* can be attacked:
- **Internet Access** - If your BCS is connected to the Internet, your network has already been *scanned* and *mapped*.
- **Wireless Network** - If you use *wireless devices* on your BCS, it has already been *scanned* and *mapped*.
- **Insider Threat** - Deliberate or inadvertent activity.
- **Direct-Access Attack** - Gaining physical access to a BCS network device.
- **Removable Media** - USB, floppy, CD, laptop, anything that can connect directly to a BCS network device.
- **Email** - *Malware* delivered by phishing email such as a *virus, Trojan horse, worm*.
- **Other Networks** - A connection to the corporate enterprise network can be one way to get into the BCS.
- **Supply Chain** - If it's made overseas, it's probably got some hidden program you'll never find.
- **Improper Installation or Usage** - Deliberate or inadvertent activity.
- **Theft of Equipment** - Lose a vital piece of equipment and your system can be left defenseless.

- **Cyber-Drone** – An aerial drone can monitor a building seeking wireless signals, such as from network printers.
- **Other** - Whatever I left out.

Aurora Vulnerability Cyber-Physical Attack - In 2007, the Idaho National Laboratory (INL) conducted a test to demonstrate how a cyber-physical attack could destroy physical components of the electric grid. INL used a computer program to rapidly open and close a diesel generator's circuit breakers out of phase from the rest of the grid. Every time the breakers were closed, the torque from the synchronization caused the generator to bounce and shake, eventually causing parts of the generator to be ripped apart and sent flying as far as 80 feet. This vulnerability can be mitigated by preventing out-of-phase opening and closing of the circuit breakers. A cyber-physical attack that takes down the commercial power grid will cause a rise in mortality rates as health and safety systems fail, a drop in trade as ports shut down, and disruption to transport and infrastructure.

Auto-Hacking Attack - An easy-to-use device with the *auto-hacking function* will hack into a *Wi-Fi network* without a computer. Simply turn on the device, select a network and the device will hack it automatically. It is a standalone machine and does not require boot from disc or computer.

Baby Monitor Cyber-Physical Attack - Internet-connected baby monitors allow parents to monitor a child's crib. They seldom encrypt the video stream and can be easily hacked because of inadequate security features. A baby monitor can also be used as an attack vector to penetrate a home's wireless network and monitor other activity. This is a fairly simple hack made possible by finding a device on the same frequency as target device. High-end baby monitors have adjustable frequencies and people tend to continue to use default or simple passwords.

Backdoor - A hidden method for bypassing normal computer authentication. Two types are:
1. **Beachhead Backdoors** - have basic features to retrieve files, gather system information, and trigger the execution of other capabilities.
2. **Standard Backdoors** - communicate using HTTP protocol to blend in with legitimate web traffic or a custom protocol and give an intruder the ability to upload/download, modify/delete/execute programs, modify the registry, capture keystrokes, harvest passwords, take screenshots, and more.

Backtracking Cyber-Attack - Also called a *directory traversal*, attack consists of exploiting insufficient security validation / sanitization of user-supplied input file names, so that characters representing "traverse to parent directory" are passed through to the file *APIs*. The goal is to use an affected application to gain unauthorized access to the file system. This attack exploits a lack of security (the software is acting exactly as it is supposed to) as opposed to exploiting a *bug* in the code. Also, known as the *../ (dot dot slash) attack*, *path traversal*, and *directory climbing*. Some forms of this attack are also *canonicalization attacks*.

Baselining - Monitoring building controls system to determine typical utilization patterns so that deviations can be detected.

Basin Heater Cyber-Physical Attack - An electric immersion heater is installed in a *cooling tower* to prevent the cold water basin from completely freezing over during shutdown or standby. It is NOT designed to prevent icing during operation. A *cracker* can cause the cooling tower to freeze up in Winter by shutting down the unit or cutting power to the basin heater. A *cracker* can also turn the basin heater on in Summer to reduce the efficiency of the unit and run up energy costs.

Behavior Monitoring - Observing activities of users, information systems, and processes and measuring the activities against organizational policies and rule, baselines of normal activity, thresholds, and trends.

Birthday Attack - A type of *cryptographic attack* that exploits the mathematics behind the birthday problem in probability theory. This attack can be used to abuse communication between two or more parties because *digital signatures* can be susceptible to a birthday attack. The attack depends on the higher likelihood of collisions found between random attack attempts and a fixed degree of permutations. Given a function f, the goal of the attack is to find two different inputs x1, x2 such that f(x1) = f(x2). Such a pair x1, x2 is called a *collision*. As an example, consider the scenario in which a teacher with a class of 30 students asks for everybody's birthday, to determine whether any two students have the same birthday (corresponding to a hash collision). Intuitively, this chance may seem small. If the teacher picked a specific day (say September 16), then the chance that at least one student was born on that specific day is about 7.9%. However, the probability that at least one student has the same birthday as any other student is around 70%.

Bit-Flipping Attack - An attack on a *cryptographic cipher* in which the attacker can change the *ciphertext* in such a way as to result in a predictable change of the plaintext, although the attacker is not able to learn the plaintext itself. Note that this type of attack is not directly against the cipher itself (as cryptanalysis of it would be), but against a particular message or series of messages. The attack is especially dangerous when the attacker knows the format of the message. In such a situation, the attacker can turn it into a similar message, but one in which some important information is altered. For example, a change in the destination address might alter the message route in a way that will force re-encryption with a weaker cipher, thus possibly making it easier for an attacker to decipher the message.

Black Box Attack - Attacker disconnects an ATM and attaches a computer to command the ATM to dispense cash.

BlackHole Exploit Kit - *Crimeware* sold that exploits Web-browser vulnerabilities.

Blended Threat Attack - A hostile action to spread malicious code via multiple methods. For example, sending a malicious URL by email, with text that encourages the recipient to click the link, is a *Blended Threat attack*. SOURCE: CNSSI-4009

Blind SQL Injection (BSQLI) Attack - Blind SQL (*Structured Query Language*) injection is a type of *SQL Injection attack* that asks the database true or false questions and determines the answer based on the applications response. This attack is often used when the web application is configured to show generic error messages, but has not mitigated the code that is vulnerable to *SQL injection*. When an attacker exploits SQL injection, sometimes the web application displays error messages from the database complaining that the SQL Query's syntax is incorrect. Blind SQL injection is nearly identical to normal *SQL Injection*, the only difference being the way the data is retrieved from the database. When the database does not output data to the web page, an attacker is forced to steal data by asking the database a series of true or false questions. This makes exploiting the SQL injection vulnerability more difficult, but not impossible.

Blue Box - A blue box is a tool that emerged in the 1960s and '70s; it allowed users to route their own calls to place free telephone calls. A related device, the *black box* enabled one to receive calls which were free to the caller. The blue box is no longer used as modern switching systems are now digital and do not use *in-band signaling*.

Bluesnarfing Attack - *Bluesnarfing* is a threat of access of information through unauthorized means. *Crackers* can gain access to the information and data on a *Bluetooth*-enabled phone using the wireless technology of the *Bluetooth* without alerting the user of the phone.

Boot Record Infector Attack - *Malware* that inserts malicious code into the *boot sector* of a disk.

Bot - A software application that runs automated tasks over the Internet. Bots perform tasks that are both simple and repetitive at a much faster rate than a human.

Botnet Attack - A group of computers taken over by malicious software and controlled across a network.

Brute-Force Attack - This type of cyber-attack is typically used as an end-all method to crack a difficult password. A brute-force attack is executed when an attacker tries to use all possible combinations of letters, numbers, and symbols to enter a correct password. Programs exist that help a *cracker* achieve this, such as *Zip Password Cracker Pro*. Any password can be cracked using the brute-force method, but it can take a very long time. The longer and more intricate a password is, the longer it will take a computer to try all of the possible combinations.

Buffer Overflow - A condition at an interface under which more input can be placed into a buffer or data holding area than the capacity allocated, overwriting other information. *Crackers* exploit such a condition to crash a system or to insert specially crafted code that allows them to gain control of the system. 4009 Buffer overruns are more easily exploited on *Windows* platforms such as x86 and x64, which use calling conventions that store the return address of a *function call* on the *stack*.

Cache Cramming Attack - The technique of tricking a browser to run cached *Java code* from the local disk, instead of the Internet zone, so it runs with less restrictive permissions.

Cache Poisoning - Malicious or misleading data from a remote name server is saved [cached] by another name server. Typically used with *DNS* cyber-attacks.

Cache Stampede Attack - A type of *cascading failure* that can occur when building control systems with caching mechanisms come under very high load. Sometimes also called *dog-piling*.

Cain & Abel - A tool for cracking *encrypted passwords* or *network keys*. It uses *network sniffing, Dictionary, Brute-Force* and *Cryptanalysis* attacks, *cache uncovering* and *routing protocol analysis* methods.

Call Back Attack - One of the first things a *cracker* does when he gets into a BCS is install a routine with automatic call back in case the system is disconnected so he can reestablish connection when system is *rebooted.*

Canonicalization Cyber-Attack - Different forms of input that resolve to the same standard name (the canonical name), is referred to as *canonicalization.* Code is particularly susceptible to *canonicalization* issues if it makes security decisions based on the name of a resource that is passed to the program as input. Files, paths, and URLs are resource types that are vulnerable to *canonicalization* because in each case there are many different ways to represent the same name. This attack exploits a lack of security (the software is acting exactly as it is supposed to) as opposed to exploiting a *bug* in the code. Recommendation: Avoid input file names where possible and instead use *absolute file paths* that cannot be changed by the end user.

Catfish - Someone who pretends to be someone they're not using Facebook or other social media to create false identities, particularly to pursue deceptive online romances.

Chain/Loop Attack - A chain of connections through many nodes as the *attacker moves across multiple nodes* to hide his origin and identity. In case of a *loop attack*, the chain of connections is in a loop making it more difficult to track down his origin.

Cinderella Attack - A cyber-attack that disables security software by manipulating the network internal clock time so a security *software license* expires prematurely rendering the target network vulnerable to cyber-attack.

Click-Jacking - Concealing *hyperlinks* beneath legitimate clickable content which, when clicked, causes a user to unknowingly perform actions, such as downloading *malware,* or sending your ID to a site. Numerous click-jacking scams have employed "*Like*" and "*Share*" buttons on social networking sites. Disable *scripting* and *iframes* in whatever Internet browser you use. SOURCE: FBI Internet Social Networking Risks

Collision Attack - A collision occurs when multiple systems transmit simultaneously on the same wire.

Computer Network Attack (CNA) - Actions taken through the use of computer networks to disrupt, deny, degrade, or destroy information resident in computers and computer networks, or the computers and networks themselves.
SOURCE: CNSSI-4009 A category of *"fires"* employed for offensive purposes in which actions are taken through the use of computer networks to disrupt, deny, degrade, manipulate, or destroy information resident in the target information system or computer networks, or the systems/networks themselves. The ultimate intended effect is not necessarily on the target system itself, but may support a larger effort, such as information operations or counter-terrorism, e.g., altering or spoofing specific communications or gaining or denying access to adversary communications or logistics channels. The term *"fires"* means the use of weapon systems to create specific lethal or nonlethal effects on a target.

CMMS Cyber-Attack - Unfortunately, a *Computerized Maintenance Management System* (CMMS) depends heavily on connectivity to the Internet as well as wireless communications to work efficiently. Building maintenance personnel are notified by the CMMS when equipment needs attention such as when a pump or valve malfunctions by generating and sending a work order to a mobile device. Personnel can access information wirelessly such as past maintenance history, preventive maintenance performed, all the specifications for the device including capacity, normal operating parameters and even whether spare parts are on hand and where they are located in the storage room. Some CMMS databases include *tenant information* such as who requested maintenance, the room number and telephone number. Some databases contain information such as security clearance for staff, labor rates, vacation schedule and contact information. The CMMS would be a great tool to target maintenance personnel for spear phishing attacks.

When a *cracker* breaks into the CMMS, he can see a great deal of information about the building and how it is operated. A *cracker* can see which pieces of equipment are *high-priority assets,* which can be considered *safety hazards* and the *trigger points for failure alarms* and *automatic shutdown.* A *cracker* can see whether spare parts are on hand so he can target equipment that would take longer to repair. Another thing to consider is that the CMMS is typically tied directly to the BCS network making the CMMS a possible attack vector for *crackers.*

Computer Virus Attack - A program that "infects" computer systems in much the same way, as a biological virus infects humans. The typical virus "reproduces" by making copies of itself and inserting them into the code of other programs—either in systems software or in application programs.

Congestion Collapse Attack - A condition that a *packet-switched* computer network can reach, when little or no useful communication is happening due to congestion. Generally, occurs at *"choke points"* in the network, where the total incoming traffic to a *node* exceeds the outgoing bandwidth.

Cookie - Data exchanged between an HTTP server and a browser (a client of the server) to store state information on the client side and retrieve it later for server use. An HTTP server, when sending data to a client, may send along a cookie, which the client retains after the HTTP connection closes. A server can use this mechanism to maintain persistent client-side state information for HTTP-based applications, retrieving the state information in later connections.

Corruption - A threat action that undesirably alters system operation by adversely modifying system functions or data.

Counter-electronics High-powered Microwave Advanced Missile Project (CHAMP) - A missile that can shut down computer systems and other nearby electronic systems from the sky through targeted emission of microwaves.

Covert Channel Attack - An unauthorized communication path that manipulates a communications medium in an unexpected, unconventional, or unforeseen way in order to transmit information without detection by anyone other than the entities operating the covert channel. SOURCE: CNSSI-4009

Crap Flooding - Posting nonsensical or repetitive postings online making it difficult for legitimate users to read other postings and suppressing relevant content.

Crimeware - Malicious software designed to carry out illegal online activity. A class of *malware* designed to automate cybercrime.

Cross-Domain Navigation Attack - Web browsers allow one document to navigate to other, non-same-origin windows to arbitrary URLs. The targeted window contains a well-formed HTML document with a resource served with the *Content-Disposition: attachment header*. Instead of the download supposedly served from a *trusted site*, it is in reality supplied by the attacker. In this attack, the address bar of the targeted window will not be updated at all - but a *rogue download* prompt will appear on the screen, attached to the targeted document. *Frame gadgets, games, advertisements* from third-party sources and even *HTML5 sandboxed frames* could permit the initiation of *rogue downloads*.

Cross-Site Scripting (XSS) Attack - A type of computer security vulnerability typically found in Web applications. XSS vulnerabilities enable attackers to *inject client-side script* (typically *Java*) into *Web pages* viewed by other users. A cross-site scripting vulnerability may be used by attackers to bypass access controls such as the same-origin policy. The effect may range from a petty nuisance to a significant security risk, depending on the sensitivity of the data handled by the vulnerable site and the nature of any security mitigation implemented by the site's owner.

Cross-Site Request Forgery (CSRF) - A type of malicious exploit of a website where unauthorized commands are transmitted from a user that the website trusts. Unlike *cross-site scripting* (XSS), which exploits the trust a user has for a particular site, CSRF exploits the trust that a site has in a user's *browser*. CSRF tricks a victim's computer into running malicious code. For example: Customers of a bank in Mexico were attacked in early 2008 with an *image tag* in email. The link in the *image tag* changed the *DNS* entry for the bank in their *ADSL router* to point to a malicious website impersonating the bank. Also, known as *one-click attack* or *session riding*.

CryptoDefense Malware Attack - One type of *Ransomware*. Paying a ransom does not guarantee a victim will be able to access the data again and in many cases this doesn't happen.

CryptoLocker Trojan Attack - A *ransomware* program distributed by email attachments.

Cyber-Attack - An attack initiated from a computer against a BCS, ICS or SCADA system or individual computer that compromises the integrity or availability of the controls system, information stored on it, or the equipment controlled by it. An attack to commit a *Cyber-Crime* is considered a Cyber-Attack. Cyber-attacks are broken down into two categories:

1. **Syntactic attacks** are straight forward; it is considered malicious software which includes *viruses, worms* and *Trojan horses*.
2. **Semantic attack** is the modification and dissemination of correct and incorrect information. Information modified could have been done without the use of computers even though new opportunities can be found by using them. To set someone into the wrong direction or to cover your tracks through dissemination of incorrect information.

Cyber-Attack (Untargeted & Targeted) - In **un-targeted attacks**, attackers <u>indiscriminately</u> target as many devices, services or users as possible. They do not care about who the victim is as there will be a number of machines or services with vulnerabilities. In a **targeted attack**, your organization is singled out because the attacker has a specific interest in your business, or has been paid to target <u>your system</u>. The groundwork for the attack could take months so that a *cracker* can find the best route to deliver the exploit directly to your systems (or users). A targeted attack is often more damaging than an un-targeted one because it has been specifically tailored to attack <u>your</u> systems, processes or personnel, in the office and sometimes at home.

Cyber Attack Tree - A conceptual diagram showing how a computer system might be attacked by describing the threats and possible cyber-attacks to realize those threats. Cyber-attack trees lend themselves to defining an information assurance strategy and are increasingly being applied to industrial control systems and the electric power grid. Executing a strategy changes the cyber-attack tree. There are at least **150** ways to attack a BCS.

Cyber Booby Trap - When a *cracker* embeds *malware* designed to be triggered by actions of the building maintenance staff. For example: the initial indication of a cyber-physical attack may be that the *cracker* turned off the water to a boiler. The maintenance personnel in the control room are unaware that the *malware* also pumped all the water out of the boiler and turned up the heat. Once the boiler is superheated, the action of turning on the water triggers an explosion. The *cracker* needed the triggering action by building maintenance personnel to initiate the damage. Before turning the water back on, maintenance personnel should make sure the power to the boiler is not turned on by manually checking the boiler and NOT rely on the BCS that has probably been rendered unreliable by the *cracker*. Also, the boiler should be *purged* before it comes back on line.

Cybercasing - The process by which a criminal can anonymously monitor a potential victim by watching as they sequentially upload valuable data about their possessions and their current geographical location (*geo-tag*).

Cyber Campaign - Denotes the time during which a given cyber force conducts a series of planned and coordinated cyber-attacks or other *Cyber Operations* in a given network environment (sometimes referred to as the "*NEO*", *Network Environment of Operation*). A cyber campaign may be executed by either a single actor, or as a combined effort of multiple actors. A cyber campaign is a series of related cyber operations aimed towards a single, specific, strategic objective or result. A cyber campaign may take place over the course of just a few days or weeks, or it can last several months or years.

Cyber-Collection - Refers to the use of *cyber-warfare* techniques in order to conduct espionage. *Cyber-collection* activities typically rely on the insertion of malware into a targeted network or computer in order to scan for, collect and exfiltrate sensitive information. *Cyber-collection* started as far back as 1996, when widespread deployment of Internet connectivity to government and corporate systems gained momentum. Since that time, there have been numerous cases of such activity. In addition to the *state sponsored* examples, *cyber-collection* has also been used by organized crime for identity and e-banking theft and by corporate spies.
Common functionality of cyber-collection systems include:
- **Data Scan**: Local and network storage are scanned to find and copy files of interest, these are often documents, spreadsheets, design files such as *Autocad* files and system files such as the password file.
- **Capture Location**: *GPS, Wi-Fi*, network information and other attached sensors are used to determine the location and movement of the infiltrated device.
- **Bug**: The device *microphone* can be activated in order to *record audio*. Likewise, audio streams intended for the local speakers can be intercepted at the device level and recorded.
- **Hidden Private Networks** that bypass the corporate network security. A computer that is being spied upon can be plugged into a legitimate corporate network that is heavy monitored for *malware* activity and at same time belongs to a private *Wi-Fi* network outside of the company network that is *leaking confidential information* off of an employee's computer. A computer like this is easily set up by a *double-agent* working in the IT department by install a second *Wireless card* in a computer and special software to remotely monitor an employee's computer through this second interface card without

them being aware of a *side-band communication channel* pulling information off of his computer.

- **Camera**: The device cameras can be activated in order to covertly *capture images* or *video*.
- **Keylogger and Mouse Logger**: The *malware* agent can capture each *keystroke, mouse movement* and *click* that the target user makes. Combined with *screen grabs*, this can be used to obtain passwords that are entered using a virtual on-screen keyboard.
- **Screen Grabber**: The *malware* agent can take periodic screen capture images. In addition to showing sensitive information that may not be stored on the machine, such as *e-banking* balances and encrypted web mail, these can be used in combination with the key and *mouse logger* data to determine access credentials for other Internet resources.
- **Encryption**: Collected data is usually encrypted at the time of capture and may be transmitted live or stored for later *exfiltration*. Likewise, it is common practice for each specific operation to use specific encryption and polymorphic capabilities of the *cyber-collection agent* in order to ensure that detection in one location will not compromise others.
- **Bypass Encryption**: Because the *malware* agent operates on the target system with all the access and rights of the user account of the target or system administrator, encryption is bypassed. For example, interception of audio using the microphone and audio output devices enables the malware to capture to both sides of an encrypted *Skype* call.
- **Exfiltration**: *Cyber-collection agents* usually exfiltrate the captured data in a discrete manner, often waiting for high web traffic and disguising the transmission as secure web browsing. *USB flash drives* have been used to exfiltrate information from *air gap* protected systems. *Exfiltration* systems often involve the use of *reverse proxy systems* that *anonymize* the receiver of the data.
- **Replicate**: Agents may replicate themselves onto other media or systems, for example an agent may infect files on a writable network share or install themselves onto *USB drives* in order to infect computers protected by an *air gap* or otherwise not on the same network.
- **Manipulate Files and File Maintenance**: *Malware* can be used to erase traces of itself from log files. It can also download and install modules or updates as well as data files. This function may also be used to place "evidence" on the target system, e.g. to insert child pornography onto the computer of a politician or to manipulate votes on an electronic vote counting machine.

- **Combination Rules**: Some agents are very complex and are able to combine the above features in order to provide very targeted intelligence collection capabilities. For example, the use of *GPS* bounding boxes and microphone activity can be used to turn a smart phone into a *"smart bug"* that intercepts conversations only within the office of a target.
- **Compromised cellphones**: Since, modern cellphones are increasingly similar to general purpose computer, these cellphones are vulnerable to the same cyber-collect attacks as computer systems, and are vulnerable to leak extremely sensitive conversational and location information to an attacker. Leaking of cellphone *GPS* location and conversational information to an attacker has been reported in a number of recent *cyber-stalking* cases where the attacker was able to use the victim's *GPS* location to call nearby businesses and police authorities to make false allegations against the victim depending on his location, this can range from telling the restaurant staff information to tease the victim, or making false witness against the victim. For instance, if the victim were parked in a large parking lot the attackers may call and state that they saw drug or violence activity going on with a description of the victim and directions to their *GPS* location. Of course, plugging a *cell phone* into a computer USB <u>to recharge the battery</u> can infect the computer.

Cyber-Drone - A cyber-drone can carry lightweight but powerful hacking platforms like *Wi-Fi Pineapple* and *Raspberry Pi*, packaged with an external battery pack and cellular connection, for powerful eavesdropping and man-in-the-middle attacks. A cyber-drone (or a swarm) can search for *Wi-Fi wireless* networks connected to a *BCS* at a facility and hack into networks when they are found. A cyber-drone can fly outside a skyscraper and find vulnerable networks with minimal interference. For example, a cyber-drone can land on a roof and target *wireless printers* because they often are the weak link in a company's wireless network. Wireless printers are typically supplied with the *Wi-Fi* connection open by default, and many companies forget to close this hole when they add the device to their *Wi-Fi* networks. This open connection potentially provides an access point for outsiders to connect to a *BCS* network. It is also possible for a cyber-drone to shut down computer systems and other nearby electronic systems from the sky through targeted emission of microwaves.

Anti-drone technology is beginning to come on the market for *WLAN* customers as cyber-drones become attached to more verified network attacks. *Fluke Networks* has released the first *cyber-drone detection signature* as an update to its *AirMagnet Enterprise* wireless *IDS/IPS* product that alerts customers to drone-specific signals. Cyber-drones are controlled via an ad hoc network and *AirMagnet* can detect the *command-and-control signaling*. The *AirMagnet* also can detect *video transmission* streams. Once alerted, the network administrator can either attempt to locate the drone and its operator, or take *RF* or *WLAN* system-level countermeasures.

Cyber Event - An observable occurrence that raises the suspicion that a cyber-incident may be occurring. Cyber events fall into 4 categories:
- **True Positive** – Something bad happened and the *NIDS* caught it.
- **True Negative** – The event is benign and no alert was generated.
- **False Positive** – The *NIDS* alert sounded, but the event was not malicious.
- **False Negative** – Something bad happened, but the *NIDS* did not catch it.

Cyber-Incident - Actions taken through the use of computer networks that result in an actual or potentially adverse effect on an information system and/or the information residing therein. SOURCE: CNSSI-4009 The difference between a *"cyber-incident"* and a *"cyber-event"* is that you are obligated to report a *cyber-incident* because it is now a law enforcement issue. A *cyber-event* merely raises the suspicion that an incident may be occurring.

Cyber-Infiltration - There are several common ways to infect or access the target:
- **An Injection Proxy** is a system that is placed upstream from the target individual or company, usually at the Internet service provider, that injects malware into the targets system. For example, an innocent download made by the user can be injected with the *malware executable* on the fly so that the target system then is accessible to *crackers*.
- **Spear Phishing**: A carefully crafted e-mail is sent to the target in order to entice them to install the malware via a *Trojan* document or a *drive by attack* hosted on a web server compromised or controlled by the *malware* owner.
- **Surreptitious Entry** may be used to infect a system. In other words, the spies carefully break into the target's office and install the *malware* on the target's system.
- **An Upstream monitor** or *sniffer* is a device that can intercept and view the data transmitted by a target system. Usually this device is placed at the Internet Service Provider. The *Carnivore* system is a

famous example of this type of system. Based on the same logic as a telephone intercept, this type of system is of limited use today due to the widespread use of encryption during data transmission.

- **A wireless infiltration** system can be used in proximity of the target when the target is using wireless technology. This is usually a laptop based system that impersonates a *Wi-Fi* or *3G* base station to capture the target systems and relay requests upstream to the Internet. Once the target systems are on the network, the system then functions as an *Injection Proxy* or as an *Upstream Monitor* in order to infiltrate or monitor the target system.
- **A USB Key** preloaded with the malware infector may be given to or dropped at the target site. Also, called a Rubber Ducky.

Cyber-Infrastructure - Includes electronic information and communications systems and services and the information contained in these systems and services. Information and communications systems and services are composed of all hardware and software that process, store, and communicate information, or any combination of all of these elements. Processing includes the creation, access, modification, and destruction of information. Storage includes paper, magnetic, electronic, and all other media types. Communications include sharing and distribution of information. For example: computer systems; control systems (e.g., supervisory control and data acquisition–SCADA); networks, such as the Internet; and cyber services (e.g., managed security services) are part of cyber-infrastructure. SOURCE: NISTIR 7628

Cyber Operational Preparation of the Environment (C-OPE) - Non-intelligence enabling functions within *cyberspace* conducted to plan and prepare for potential follow-on military operations. C-OPE includes, but is not limited to identifying data, system/network configurations, or physical structures connected to or associated with the network or system (to include software, ports, and assigned network address ranges or other identifiers) for the purpose of determining system vulnerabilities; and actions taken to assure future access and/or control of the system, network, or data during anticipated hostilities.

Cyber-Physical Attack - A classic cyber-physical attack would be when a *cracker* is able to damage building equipment by sending destructive commands over the BCS to the equipment that change the *setpoints* above dangerous levels for which the equipment has not been designed, such as too high pressure or dangerously high temperature. A cyber-physical attack is an attack that does actual physical damage to vulnerable physical systems and equipment.

Cyber-Physical Attack Engineering - Designing an attack scenario to exploit a particular physical process requires a solid engineering background and in-depth *destructive* knowledge of the target SCADA system. Hacking a chemical plant, for example requires knowledge of physics, chemistry and engineering, as well as a great deal about how the network is laid out, and a keen understanding of process-aware defensive systems. This represents a high (but not insurmountable) barrier to entry to garden-variety script kiddies, but is not a major obstacle for a foreign intelligence service.

Cyber Tools -
- **Commodity Capability** - Cyber tools and techniques openly available on the Internet (off-the-shelf) that are relatively simple to use. This includes tools designed for security specialists (such as building control system penetration testers) that can also be used by attackers as they are specifically designed to scan for publicly known vulnerabilities in operating systems and applications. Poison Ivy is a good example of a commodity tool; it is a readily available Remote Access Tool (RAT) that has been widely used for a number of years.
- **Bespoke Capability** - Cyber tools and techniques that are developed and used for specific purposes, and thus require more specialist knowledge. This could include malicious code ('exploits') that take advantage of software vulnerabilities (or bugs) that are not yet known to vendors or anti-malware companies, often known as *'zero-day'* exploits. It could also include undocumented software features, or poorly designed applications. Bespoke capabilities usually become commodity capabilities once their use has been discovered, sometimes within a few days. By their very nature, the availability of bespoke tools is not advertised as once released they become a commodity. SOURCE: CERT-UK

Cyborg Unplug - A plug-and-play network appliance that automatically detects and disconnects a range of Internet-connected surveillance devices including *Dropcam*, *Google Glass* and *Wi-Fi-enabled drones* by breaking uploads and streams. It sniffs the air for wireless signatures from devices known to pose a risk to personal privacy, Cyborg Unplug will disconnect them, stopping them from streaming video, audio and data to the Internet and it sends an email alert. Most wireless devices used for surveillance; stream data to a machine on the Internet or in a nearby room allowing for remote surveillance while ensuring the offending device contains no evidence (files) of the abuse.

Data Breach - The unauthorized movement or disclosure of sensitive information to a party, usually outside the organization, that is not authorized to have or see the information.

Data Loss Attack - The result of unintentionally or accidentally deleting data, forgetting where it is stored, or exposure to an unauthorized party.

Deauthorization Cyber-Attack - This attack is launched when a *cracker* is able to send a command (usually over Wi-Fi) to legitimate users instructing them to log off (presumably to perform system maintenance). The *cracker* then harvests passwords and log in credentials when users log back on.

Defacement Attack - The method of modifying the content of a website in such a way that it becomes "vandalized" or embarrassing to the website owner.

Deauthentication Packet Attack - This attack sends disassociating packets to one or more clients which are currently associated with a particular Wi-Fi access point thereby breaking the connection. The deauthentication packets are sent directly from a PC to the clients, so the attacker must be physically close enough to the clients for wireless transmissions to reach them.

Denial of Service Attack (DoS) - A cyber-attack meant to make a computer resource unavailable to its intended users. There are multiple ways to execute a DoS attack. Some of the different forms of execution include:
1. **Teardrop** - Sending irregularly shaped network data packets.
2. **Buffer Overflow** - Flooding a server with an overwhelming amount data.
3. **Smurf** - Tricking computers to reply to a fake request, causing much traffic.
4. **Physical** - Disrupting a physical connection, such as a cable or power source.

Diagnostic Server Attacks - An attacker can execute the following attacks without any authentication required while maintaining stealthiness such as remote memory dump, remote memory patch, remote calls to functions and remote task management.

Dictionary Attack - A dictionary attack takes place when an attacker utilizes a dictionary in an attempt to crack a password. Essentially, words from the dictionary are inputted into the password field to try to guess the password. Programs and tools exist that allow hackers to easily try various combinations of words in the dictionary against a user's password. Because of the dictionary attack, it is recommended to use passwords that do not contain simple words that can be found in a dictionary.

Digital Picture Frame Attack - Some digital picture frames manufactured in China have been found to contain a virus that steals passwords and financial information, blocks security and replicates when loading pictures from a home computer.

Direct-Access Attack - A direct-access attack simply means gaining physical access to the computer or its part and performing various functions or installing various types of devices to compromise security. The attacker can install software loaded with *worm*s or download important data, using portable devices.

Directory Climbing Cyber-Attack - Also called a *directory traversal*, attack consists of exploiting insufficient security validation / sanitization of user-supplied input file names, so that characters representing "traverse to parent directory" are passed through to the file APIs. The goal is to use an affected application to gain unauthorized access to the file system. This attack exploits a lack of security (the software is acting exactly as it is supposed to) as opposed to exploiting a bug in the code. Also, known as the *../ (dot dot slash) attack, path traversal* and *backtracking*. Some forms of this attack are also *canonicalization attacks*.

Disappearing Malware - *Malware* that resides only in the infected machine's random-access-memory, rather than on the hard drive, so that the malware leaves no discernible footprint once it's gone. A *fileless malware* attack is similar because no malware gets installed on the system and the *cracker* uses the existing legitimate tools on the machine such as *Microsoft Powershell* or *WMI*. Tracking *fileless* attacks is difficult, but not impossible using memory forensics techniques.

Distributed Denial of Service (DDoS) Attack - When many *UDP packets* have their source *IP address* forged to a single address, the server responds to that victim, creating a reflected *Denial of Service (DoS) Attack*. A single packet can generate tens or hundreds of times the bandwidth in its response. This is called an *amplification attack*, and when combined with a reflective *DoS attack* on a large scale, *DDoS attacks* can be conducted with relative ease.

Distributed Scans - Scans that use multiple source addresses to gather information.

DNS Forgery Attack - A *cracker* with access to a network can easily forge responses to the computer's *DNS* requests.

DNS Spoofing - A computer hacking attack, whereby data is introduced into a *Domain Name System (DNS)* resolver's cache, causing the name server to return an incorrect IP address, diverting traffic to the attacker's computer (or any other computer). Also, called *DNS cache poisoning*.

Dodging Cyber-Attack - See *Impersonation Cyber-Attack*.

Domain Hijacking Attack - An attack by which a *cracker* takes over a domain by first blocking access to the domain's *DNS server* and then putting his own server up in its place.

Doorknob-Rattling Attack - A *cracker* attempts a very few common username and password combinations on several computers resulting in very few failed login attempts. This attack can go undetected unless the data related to login failures from all the hosts are collected and aggregated to check for doorknob-rattling from any remote destination.

Drive-by Download Attack - *Malware* is installed on a person's computer or other device as soon as they visit a compromised website.

Dropper Attack - Computer malware which allows attackers to open a backdoor to install another malware program to an infected machine to implement additional functionality.

Dumpster Diving - Dumpster Diving is obtaining passwords and corporate directories by searching through discarded media.

Eavesdropping - Eavesdropping is simply listening to a private conversation which may reveal information which can provide access to a facility or network.

Elevator Attack - A *Trojan horse* can be installed on a BCS network that when activated is able to put an elevator into diagnostics mode and send it to another floor.

Emanations Analysis - Gaining direct knowledge of communicated data by monitoring and resolving a signal that is emitted by a system and that contains the data but is not intended to communicate the data.

Exfiltration - The unauthorized transfer of information from an information system.

Exploit - A technique to breach the security of a network or information system in violation of security policy. An exploit attack is basically software designed to take advantage of a flaw in the system. The attacker plans to gain easy access to a computer system and gain control, allows privilege escalation or creates a *DoS attack*.

Fileless Cyber-Attack Malware - A fileless cyber-attack uses inherent "features" built into *Windows* to turn the *operating system* against itself to compromise a computer network. The best examples are using *Windows Management Instrumentation (WMI)* and *Powershell*. *WMI* has access to every resource on the machine and can perform various tasks such as execute files, delete and copy files, or change registry values. *Powershell* is an even more powerful tool for *crackers*. Some new *fileless malware* types reside in an encrypted form in the *Windows registry hive*. *Kovter, Powelike,* and *XswKit* are *fileless registry attack malware* that destroys itself upon execution and leave no trace on the file system. *WMI* cannot be uninstalled (but it can be disabled). Since no other software needs to be installed, a *fileless attack* is nearly impossible for traditional *antivirus* tools to detect. Tracking *fileless attacks* may be difficult, but it's not impossible.

Fingerprinting Smartphones - A *New York Times* report revealed that *Uber*'s app could give *iPhones* a unique *"fingerprint"* so that the company could identify devices even if its *app* was deleted or the phone was erased entirely. *Uber* attempted to prevent *Apple*'s engineers from detecting the code by putting *Apple*'s Cupertino headquarters inside a *"geo-fence,"* so its software would appear differently when viewed in that location. *Fingerprinting* is a way to prevent fraudsters from loading *Uber* onto a stolen phone, putting in a stolen credit card, taking an expensive ride and then wiping the phone — over and over again.

Fire Sale Attack - As seen in the 2007 movie *"Live Free or Die Hard"*. A Fire Sale is an assault against a government, transportation and economy by computer hackers. Much like the more common term meaning "everything must go." Any and all computer-based systems are the objective and would destroy the modern-day life of a nation. The three stages of a fire sale are:

1. **Stage 1:** Shut down transportation systems: traffic lights, railroads, subways and airports.
2. **Stage 2:** Disable financial systems: Wall Street, banks and financial records.
3. **Stage 3:** Turn off public utility systems: electricity, gas lines, telecom and satellite systems.

FitBit Hack - *FitBit* has been shown to be hacked creating a possible cyber-attack vector that could allow *crackers* to infect any PC connected to it. A *virus* is uploaded to the *Fitbit* that uploads to your PC via *USB*.

Flame Virus - This computer virus can record *audio, screenshots, keyboard activity* and *network traffic*. It can record *Skype* conversations and can turn infected computers into *Bluetooth beacons* which attempt to download contact information from nearby Bluetooth-enabled devices. Also, known as *Flamer, Da Flame, sKyWIper*, and *Skywiper*. *Flame* supports a "kill" command which wipes all traces of the *malware* from the computer. Due to the size and complexity of the program (20 MB) it is described as "twenty times" more complicated than *Stuxnet*.

Flooding Attack - A cyber-attack that attempts to cause a failure in the security of a computer system or industrial control device by providing more input than the device can process properly.

Fork Bomb Attack - A cyber-attack that works by using the fork() call to create a new process which is a copy of the original. By doing this repeatedly, all available processes on the machine can be taken up.

Fragment Overlap Attack - A *TCP/IP Fragmentation Attack* is possible because IP allows packets to be broken down into fragments for efficient transport. The TCP packet (and its header) are carried in the *IP* packet. In this attack, the second fragment contains incorrect offset. When the packet is reconstructed, the *port number* is overwritten.

Function Pointer Attack - A buffer overflow by overwriting a function pointer or exception handler, which is subsequently executed.

Fuzzing Attack - A cyber-attack when indiscriminate data is transmitted to a server in an attempt to override controls.

Google Chrome Attacks - *Chrome* will automatically download files that it deems safe without prompting the user for a download location. *Google* deems *SCF* files as safe, having no reason to prompt the user for action.

There are many websites vulnerable to *"reflected file downloads"* that allow attackers to download files onto users' computers. In *Chrome*'s default configuration, the *SCF* file will be downloaded to the user's *Downloads folder*. Users that notice the download and go to the *Downloads folder* to inspect this suspicious file will launch the *credentials sharing attack* without their knowledge, as soon as they open the directory.

Google Docs OAuth Cyber-Attack - In the *Google Docs* scheme, the attacker created a fake version of *Google Docs* and asked for permission to read, write and access the victim's emails. By granting the *OAuth* exploit permission, users effectively gave the bad guys access to their account without needing a password. When *crackers* use *OAuth* exploits, they don't need to enter a password -- the victim duped into giving permission already did. See *Open Authorization*.

Gray Hole Attack - A type of *packet drop attack* in which a router that is supposed to relay packets instead discards them for a particular network destination, at a certain time of the day, a packet every n packets or every t seconds, or a randomly selected portion of the packets. This usually occurs from a router becoming compromised from a number of different causes. Because packets are routinely dropped from a lossy network, the packet drop attack is very hard to detect and prevent.

Headless Worm - Although the *Conficker* computer *worm* that used to command a large *botnet* was neutralized years ago prevented the people who released the worm from using it, the malicious code can still be found on infected personal computers.

Hijack Attack - Active wiretapping in which the *cracker* seizes control of a previously established communication association.

Hit Inflation Attack - A hit inflation attack is a kind of fraudulent method used by some Internet advertisement publishers to earn unjustified revenue on the click traffic they drive to the advertisers' Web sites. It is more sophisticated and harder to detect than a simple *inflation attack*.

Hybrid Attack - A cyber-attack that builds on the *dictionary attack* method by adding numerals and symbols to dictionary words.

Identity Theft - One of the most common types of cybercrime, Identity Theft is when a person purports to be some other person, with a view to creating a fraud for financial gains. When this is done online on the Internet, it is called *Online Identity Theft*. The most common source to steal identity information of others, are data breaches affecting government websites and private websites.

Impersonation Cyber-Attack - This is an attempt to fool a *facial recognition system* (FRS) and allow an attacker to evade recognition or impersonate another individual in a manner that is imperceptible. This is not to be confused with simply wearing a mask or an excessive amount of makeup in order to evade a surveillance system which is easily detected by a human. This refers to manipulating the physical state that a *Machine Learning (ML)* algorithm is analyzing rather than the digitized representation of this state. *Neural Networks* have been shown to be misled by mildly perturbing inputs (6.5%) because of the non-flexibility of the classification models. There are two categories of these attacks: *dodging* and *impersonation*. In a *dodging* attack, the individual seeks to have his face misidentified as any other *arbitrary* face (such as by individuals seeking to protect their privacy against excessive CCTV surveillance). In an *impersonation* attack, the attacker seeks to have a face recognized as a *specific* other face such as a legitimate laptop user. *Dodging attacks* are easier to implement than impersonation attacks by using facial accessories (such as eyeglasses), however specially printed eyeglass frames have been proven successful in the lab for *impersonation attacks*.

Indirect Attack - A cyber-attack launched from a third-party computer making it difficult to track the origin of the attack.

Inference Attack - A data mining technique performed by analyzing data in order to illegitimately gain knowledge about a subject or database. Sensitive information can be considered leaked if an adversary can infer its real value with a high degree of confidence.

Input Validation Attack - A cyber-attack when a *cracker* intentionally sends unusual input in the hopes of confusing an application.

Insider Attack - An entity inside the security perimeter that is authorized to access system resources, but uses them in a way not approved by those who granted the authorization. In addition to intentional violators, other types of insiders are:
1. **Exploited insiders** may be "tricked" by external parties into providing data or passwords they shouldn't.
2. **Careless insiders** may simply press the wrong key and accidentally delete or modify critical information.

Insider Threat - The ability of a trusted insider to bypass or defeat security safeguards or otherwise adversely affect national security.

Intellectual Property Theft - A theft of copyrighted material where it violates the copyrights and the patents. A cybercrime intended to steal trade secrets, patents and research. Theft of an idea, plan or methodology.

IP Camera Cyber-Attack - Hacking into a *BCS* thru an *IP* camera as the attack vector.

IP Flood Attack - *Denial of Service* attack that sends a host more "ping" packets than the protocol can handle.

Interruption - An outage caused by the failure of one or more communications links with entities outside of the local facility.

Jamming Attack - An attack in which a device is used to emit electromagnetic energy on a wireless network's frequency to make it unusable. SOURCE: SP 800-48

Keystroke Injection Attack - A USB thumb drive (called a *"Rubber Ducky"*) containing malware that fools a computer into thinking it is a keyboard. Whether it be a *Windows, Mac, Linux* or *Android* device, any *USB* device claiming to be a *Keyboard HID* (Human Input Device) will be automatically detected and accepted by most modern operating systems. By taking advantage of this inherent trust with *scripted keystrokes* at speeds beyond 1,000 words per minute traditional countermeasures can be bypassed. A *cracker* will change the *VID/PID* on a thumb drive to fool the computer into thinking it is another device, with the intent to load *malicious payload*, either a file or *scripted code*. This is very effective because most anti-virus software is looking at *files*, not *scripted language* entered by keyboard.

Keystroke Logger Attack - A program designed to record which keys are pressed on a computer keyboard used to obtain passwords or encryption keys and thus bypass other security measures.

Kinetic Cyber-Attack - A violent cyber-physical attack that is intended to cause physical damage in the real world to people, buildings, equipment, infrastructure or a nation's way of life. Not a virtual attack or theft of data.

Kovter Cyber-Attack - A *fileless registry attack malware* that destroys itself upon execution and leaves no trace on the file system.

Laboratory Attack - Use of sophisticated *signal recovery equipment* in a laboratory environment to recover information from data storage media. SOURCE: SP 800-88; CNSSI-4009

Laptop Webcam Hack - Most laptops are equipped with a built-in *webcam* and *microphone* and both can be hacked. An attacker can listen in or watch you work at your laptop without your knowledge. This is a fairly simple hack made possible by *Trojan horse malware* called *"Blackshades"* that even a *script kiddie* can master.

Like-Jacking Attack - Occurs when criminals post fake Facebook "like" buttons to webpages. Users who click the button don't "like" the page, but instead download *malware*.

Link-Jacking Attack - This is a practice used to redirect one website's links to another which *crackers* use to redirect users from trusted websites to malware infected websites that hide drive-by downloads or other types of infections.

Link Service Access Point (LSAP) - An LSAP is a *threebyte header* including a destination, a source field, and a control field. A *service access point* is a label for network endpoints in *OSI* networks.

Logic Bomb Attack - A computer code that is preset to cause a malfunction, at a later time, when a specified set of logical conditions occurs. For example, a specific social security number in a payroll system is processed and the *logic bomb* is activated, causing an improper amount of money to be printed on the check.

Macro Virus Attack - A type of malicious code that attaches itself to documents and uses the macro programming capabilities of the document's application to execute, replicate, and spread or propagate itself.

Malicious Applet Attack - A small application program that is automatically downloaded and executed and that performs an unauthorized function on an information system.

Malicious Code Attack - Program code intended to perform an unauthorized function or process that will have adverse impact on the confidentiality, integrity, or availability of a building control system. SOURCE: SP 800-53; CNSSI-4009

Malicious Logic - Hardware, firmware, or software that is intentionally included or inserted in a system to perform an unauthorized function or process that will have adverse impact on the confidentiality, integrity, or availability of an information system.

Malicious Reconnaissance - A method for actively probing or *passively monitoring* an information system for the purpose of discerning security vulnerabilities of the information system, if such method is associated with a known or suspected cybersecurity threat.

Malicious Software Attack - Any of a family of computer programs developed with the sole purpose of doing damage. Malicious code is usually *embedded* in software programs that appear to provide useful functions but, when activated by a user, cause undesirable results.

Malvertising Attack - A method whereby users download malicious code by simply clicking on a malicious advertisement placed on a website by cyber-criminals without the knowledge of the website owner. The malverts easily pass off as genuine advertisements on a website that is infected.

Malware Attack - Malicious software designed to infiltrate or damage a building control system. Software or firmware intended to perform an unauthorized process that will have adverse impact on the confidentiality, integrity, or availability of a building control system. *Malware* types include *virus, worm, Trojan horse, Root kit, spyware* and *adware* designed to infect a host. *Spyware* and some forms of *adware* are also examples of *malicious code (malware).* SOURCE: SP 800-83

Man in the Browser (MitB) Attack - A cybercriminal constructs a fake bank website and entices the user to that website. The user then inputs their credentials and the cybercriminal in turn uses the credentials to access the bank's real website. The victim is not aware they are not actually at the legitimate bank's website. The cybercriminal then has the option to either abruptly disconnect the victim and initiate fraudulent transactions themselves, or pass along the victim's banking transactions to minimize suspicion and return later to withdraw funds. The attacker can hide records of money transfers, spoof balances, and change payment details. This type of cyber-attack has been shown to be able to defeat *two-factor authentication* systems.

Man in the Middle (MITM) Attack - A cyber-attack where the attacker secretly relays and possibly alters the communication between two parties who believe they are directly communicating with each other.

Masquerade Attack - A cyber-attack in which one system entity illegitimately poses as another entity.

Mass Cyber-Attack - Researchers have shown how *BCS* and *SCADA field devices* can be attacked by *cracker*s and once *crackers* determine how a specific device can be hacked, *cracker*s may be able to launch mass attacks by leveraging the *firmware update utilities* provided by vendors. Thousands of these systems are easily accessible from the Internet, allowing *crackers* to hijack them by replacing the firmware with a malicious version. These attacks can focus on *programmable logic controllers* (PLCs), which are critical for operations or *crackers* can run ransomware attacks on thousands of victims simultaneously.

Medical Dialysis Machine Cyber-Physical Attack - A dialysis machine is designed to replace many of the kidney's important functions and restore a patient's blood to a normal, healthy balance by filtering out harmful wastes, salt and excess fluid. There are a number of things a *cracker* can do if he accesses this device. See my book *"Cybersecurity for Hospitals and Healthcare Facilities"*.

Medical Defibrillator Cyber-Physical Attack - A malicious *cracker* may be able to corrupt a Bluetooth-enabled defibrillator to deliver random shocks to a patient's heart or prevent a shock from occurring. See my book *"Cybersecurity for Hospitals and Healthcare Facilities"*.

Medical Device Data Systems (MDDS) - Medical Device Data Systems are networked hardware or software products that transfer, store, convert formats, and display medical device data, and they can be hacked. An MDDS does not modify the data or modify the display of the data, and it does not by itself control the functions or parameters of any other medical device.

Medical Device Hijack - In 2012 a *White Hat hacker* claimed he could kill a diabetic person from 300 feet away by ordering an insulin pump to deliver fatal doses of insulin. More recently, he announced he could hack pacemakers and implanted defibrillators. Researchers report that targeted hospitals are being attacked by an attack vector called *MEDJACK*. Attacking medical equipment is similar to hacking building equipment or industrial equipment. A *cracker* can attack the "**operative system**" of any machine (the part that actually performs the machine's intended function), or he can hack the **"protective system"** of a machine (the part that monitors the process for deviations from the expected results) - or he can attack both systems. When a failure of the operative system occurs, the protective system detects the failure and transfers the device into a "safe state." See my book *"Cybersecurity for Hospitals and Healthcare Facilities"*.

Medical-Grade Network (MGN) - A MGN provides the industry-specific framework required to meet healthcare's unique needs for interoperability, security, availability, productivity, and flexibility. SOURCE: Cisco Systems Inc.

Medical Image Storage Device Attack - Medical Image Storage Devices provide electronic storage and retrieval functions for medical images and they can be hacked. See my book *"Cybersecurity for Hospitals and Healthcare Facilities"*.

Medical Infusion Pump Cyber-Physical Attack - An infusion pump delivers high-risk medications and critical fluids, medication or nutrients into a patient's circulatory system. If a *cracker* can tamper with the delivery of fluids, that can have dire consequences for the patient. See my book *"Cybersecurity for Hospitals and Healthcare Facilities"*.

Medical Laser Cyber-Physical Attack - Different medical lasers are designed for a wide range of treatments and each has risks when not being used as designed. Misuse of an infrared (IR) laser that is thermal in nature may result in permanently damaged tissue. See my book *"Cybersecurity for Hospitals and Healthcare Facilities"*.

Medical Robotic Surgical Machine Cyber-Physical Attack - A is used to aid in many types of surgical procedures including: urology, cardiology, colon and rectal surgery, gynecology, neurosurgery, vascular and transplant surgery. A surgeon uses a live video feed and a computer to control the robotic arms and the end-effectors. Examples of robotic surgical attack vectors can be found in my book *"Cybersecurity for Hospitals and Healthcare Facilities"*.

Medical X-Ray Machine Cyber-Physical Attack - Medical X-Ray machines are used to take pictures of dense tissues. The radiation from X-Ray machines are highly penetrating, ionizing radiation, therefore they can be very dangerous. If a *cracker* is able to increase the dose or radiation exposure, a patient could be over-exposed to enough radiation that will result in permanent destruction of either hair or sweat glands, or whole skin with a resulting scar. See my book *"Cybersecurity for Hospitals and Healthcare Facilities"*.

Medical X-Ray Computed Tomography (CT) Scanner Cyber-Physical Attack - A CT scanner uses X-Ray images taken from different angles to produce cross-sectional (tomographic) images (virtual 'slices') of specific areas of a scanned patient, allowing the physician to see inside the patient without cutting. CT is regarded as a moderate- to high-radiation diagnostic technique, however the radiation doses received from CT scans are 100 to 1,000 times higher than conventional X-Rays. See my book *"Cybersecurity for Hospitals and Healthcare Facilities"*.

Metamorphic and Polymorphic Malware Attack - This category of malware keeps changing its code so each of its succeeding versions is different than the previous one. Metamorphic and polymorphic *malware* evades detection and conventional anti-virus programs. It is difficult to write since it requires complicated techniques.

Mobile Ad-hoc Network (MANET) Attack - These cyber-attacks slow or stop the flow of information on the building automation network. MANETs are more vulnerable to malicious attacks.

Mousetrapping - Program that prevents a user from leaving a website.

Network Outage - An interruption in system availability as a result of a communication failure affecting a network of computer terminals, processors, or workstations.

Network Tap - A hardware device which provides a way to access the data flowing across a computer network. Analogous to *phone tap* or *vampire tap*.

Night Dragon Attack - This virus targeted global oil companies with the aim of finding project details and financial information about oil and gas field exploration and bids.

Obfuscated Spam - An e-mail that has been designed to fool anti-spam software. For example, replacing one letter in the word Viagra, so it is written as "V!agra".

Off-line Attack - An attack where the *cracker* obtains some data (typically by eavesdropping on an authentication protocol run, or by penetrating a building control system and stealing security files) that he is able to analyze in a building control system of his own choosing. SOURCE: SP 800-63

Microsoft Office Zero-Day - This cyber-attack uses malware that allows attackers to silently execute code on targeted machines and secretly install malware if the user has disabled *Office Protected View*. The exploit executes automatically, making an HTTP request to the attacker's server, from where it downloads an HTML application file, disguised as an *RTF*. Attacks with this *zero-day* start with an adversary emailing a victim a *Microsoft Word* document. The *Word* document contains a booby-trapped *OLE2link object*. While the attack uses *Word* documents, *OLE2link* objects can also be embedded in other *Microsoft Office* applications, such as *Excel* and *PowerPoint*.

Online Attack - An attack against an authentication protocol where the Attacker either assumes the role of a Claimant with a genuine Verifier or actively alters the authentication channel. The goal of the attack may be to gain authenticated access or learn authentication secrets. SOURCE: SP 800-63

One-Time Password Attack - A one-time password is a code issued by a small electronic device every 30 or 60 seconds that is valid for only one login session or transaction. Online thieves have created real-time *Trojan horse* programs that can issue transactions to a bank while the account holder is online, turning the one-time password into a huge vulnerability. SOURCE: FFIEC

Operating System Command Injection (OSCI) - An attack in which the goal is execution of arbitrary commands on the host operating system via a vulnerable application. *Command injection attacks* are possible when an application passes unsafe user supplied data (forms, *cookies, HTTP* headers etc.) to a system shell. In this attack, the attacker-supplied operating system commands are usually executed with the privileges of the vulnerable application. *Command injection attacks* are possible largely due to insufficient input validation. This attack differs from *Code Injection*, in that code injection allows the attacker to add his own code that is then executed by the application. In *Code Injection*, the attacker extends the default functionality of the application without the necessity of executing system commands. Recommendation: A developer should use existing API for their language. For example (Java): Rather than use *Runtime.exec()* to issue a 'mail' command, use the available *Java API*. If no such available API exists, the developer should scrub all input for malicious characters. Implementing a positive security model would be most efficient. Typically, it is much easier to define the legal characters than the illegal characters.

Overlay Cyber Attack - Overlay malware allows attackers to create an overlay to be displayed on top of legitimate Android applications. The overlay then tricks users into entering their access credentials into a fake window that will grab and forward them to a remote attacker. According to Limor Kessem, a cybersecurity analyst with *IBM X-Force*, "Overlay malware is a criminal's Swiss Army Knife. It's flexible and effective at stealing financial credentials as well as a multitude of other types of sensitive data on an Android device." One example of this is an attack on a *connected car*. Automakers and third-party developers have released apps that turn smartphones into vehicular remote controls, allowing drivers to locate, lock, and unlock their rides with a screen tap. When the car app launches, the *overlay malware* would detect it loading and preempt it with a fake interface that steals and transmits the user's credentials. *Overlay malware* can easily be defeated. Also, see *Passive Keyless Entry*.

Overload Attack - In an overload cyber-attack, a shared resource or service is overloaded with requests to such a point that it's unable to satisfy requests from other users.

Packet Drop Attack - A type of denial-of-service attack in which a router that is supposed to relay packets instead discards them. This usually occurs from a router becoming compromised from a number of different causes. One cause mentioned in research is through a *denial-of-service* attack on the router using a known *DDoS* tool. Because packets are routinely dropped from a lossy network, the packet drop attack is very hard to detect and prevent. Also, called a *Black Hole Attack*. The malicious router can also accomplish this attack selectively, e.g. by *dropping packets* for a particular network destination, at a certain time of the day, a packet every n packets or every t seconds, or a randomly selected portion of the packets. This is called a *Gray Hole Attack*.

Page Jacking - Stealing content such as source code from a website and copying it to another website.

Parasitic Wi-Fi - It is possible to induce parasitic signals on the audio front end of voice-command-capable devices such as the *iPhone*. A *cracker* can send radio waves to any *Android or iPhone* that has *Google Now* or *Siri* enabled. The hack uses the phone's headphone cord as an antenna to convert electrical signals that appear to the phone's operating system to be audio coming from the microphone. Anything you can do through the voice interface you can do remotely and discretely through electromagnetic waves.

Pass the Hash Attack - A hacking technique that allows an attacker to authenticate to a remote server/service by using the underlying NTLM and/or LanMan hash of a user's password, instead of requiring the associated plaintext password as is normally the case. The attack exploits an implementation weakness in the authentication protocol in that the password hashes are not *salted*, and therefore remain static from session to session until the password is next changed.

Passive Attack - An actual assault perpetrated by an intentional threat source that attempts to learn or make use of information from a system, but does not attempt to alter the system, its resources, its data, or its operations.

Passive Keyless Entry - A *smart key* is an automobile's electronic access and authorization of system that allows the driver to keep the key fob pocketed when unlocking, locking and starting the vehicle. A *smart-key* system can disengage the immobilizer and activate the ignition without inserting a key in the ignition. The system works by having a series of LF (low frequency 125 kHz) transmitting antennas both inside and outside the vehicle. The *smart key* determines if it is inside or outside the vehicle by measuring the strength of the LF fields. Generally speaking, in order to start the vehicle, the *smart key* must be inside the vehicle. A *"relay station attack"* is based on the idea of reducing the long physical distance between the car and the regular car owner's *smart key* fob. By locating a relay station near the car and a second relay station close to the *smart key* fob, a *cracker* can spoof the signal from a car's wireless key fob 1000 feet away to open a vehicle's doors, and even drive the car away. The cost to build a device like this is about $22. Also, called a *relay hack*.

Passive Keyless Relay Attack - By building a pair of radio devices; one meant to be held a few feet from the victim's car, while the other is placed near the victim's key fob, *cracker*s can break into or steal a car. The first radio impersonates the car's key and pings the car's wireless entry system, triggering a signal from the vehicle that seeks a radio response from the key. Then that signal is relayed between the attackers' two radios as far as 300 feet, eliciting the correct response from the key, which is then transmitted back to the car to complete the "handshake."

Path Traversal (TRAV) Cyber-Attack - Also called a *directory traversal*, a TRAV consists of exploiting insufficient security validation /

sanitization of user-supplied input file names, so that characters representing "traverse to parent directory" are passed through to the file *APIs*. The goal is to use an affected application to gain unauthorized access to the file system. This attack exploits a lack of security (the software is acting exactly as it is supposed to) as opposed to exploiting a bug in the code. Also, known as the *../ (dot dot slash) attack*, *directory climbing*, and *backtracking*. Some forms of this attack are also *canonicalization attacks*.

Payment Card Skimmer Attack - Illegally installed device to read credit cards as customers pay.

PDF File Attack - Web-based attacks are often hiding inside a PDF file.

Pharming Attack - A sophisticated MITM attack where a user's session is redirected to a masquerading website. At the pseudo website, transactions can be mimicked and information like login credentials of a valid user can be gathered.

Phishing Attack - Tricking individuals into disclosing sensitive personal information by claiming to be a trustworthy entity in an electronic communication (e.g., Internet web sites). Phishing typically involves both social engineering and technical trickery to deceive victims into opening attached files, clicking on embedded links, and revealing sensitive information.

Phreaking - A slang term describing the activity of a culture of people who study, experiment with, or explore telecommunication systems, such as equipment and systems connected to public telephone networks.

Piggybacking Attack - Intentional access of an open Wi-Fi network without harmful intent. Some jurisdictions prohibit it, some permit it, and others are not well-defined. In the U.S., the laws vary widely between states. For example, it is a third-degree felony in the state of Florida. New York law is the most permissive. The statute against unauthorized access only applies when the network "is equipped or programmed with any device or coding system, a function of which is to prevent the unauthorized use of said computer or computer system". In other words, the use of a network would only be considered unauthorized and illegal if the network owner had enabled encryption or password protection and the user bypassed this protection, or when the owner has explicitly given notice that use of the network is prohibited. A customer of a business providing hotspot service, such as a hotel or café, is generally not considered to be piggybacking.

Ping of Death Attack - A cyber-attack that sends a large echo request packet (a "ping") with the intent of overflowing the input buffers of the destination machine causing it to crash.

Ping Scan Attack - A cyber-attack looking for machines responding to pings.

Ping Sweep Attack - A cyber-attack that pings a range of IP addresses, with the goal of finding hosts that can be probed for vulnerabilities.

PINLogger Cyber-Attack - An attack that makes it possible for a sneaky website to surreptitiously collect personal identification numbers we use to unlock an iOS or Android device or to log in to sites that are protected by two-factor authentication. PINLogger does not require the installation of any malicious apps. Depending on the browser, legitimate sites serving malicious ads or malicious content access motion and orientation sensors to guess four-digit PINs, with a 94-percent chance of success. If you open a web page and then a second web page without closing the first one, the first web page can listen in on what you type in the second web page.

Poison Ivy - A *Remote Access Tool (RAT)* designed to scan for publicly known vulnerabilities in operating systems and applications.

Poison Reverse Attack - Split horizon with poisoned reverse includes routes in updates, but sets their metrics to infinity. In effect, advertising the fact that their routes are not reachable.

Port Scanning Attack - A cyber-attack using a program to remotely determine which ports on a system are open (e.g., whether systems allow connections through those ports).

Powelike! Cyber-Attack - A fileless registry attack malware that destroys itself upon execution and leaves no trace on the file system. It is basically a Trojan that can change the settings of your computer to steal money and privacy.

Power over Ethernet (PoE) Hack - Technology that uses unused conductors on *Ethernet* cabling to power low voltage devices. Up to 44 volts 350 ma is available. *POE Plus* can provide up to 25.5 Watts. An attacker that hacks into a security network and causes a power surge on the *Ethernet* cabling may be able to cause devices to fail.

PowerShell (Fileless Attack) - Task automation and configuration management framework from *Microsoft*, consisting of a command-line shell and associated scripting language built on the *.NET Framework*. Can be used as a *Fileless Malware* cyber-attack.

Preimage Attack - In cryptography, a preimage attack on cryptographic hash functions tries to find a message that has a specific hash value. A *cryptographic hash* function should resist attacks on its preimage. Some significant preimage attacks have already been discovered, but they are not yet practical. If a practical preimage attack is discovered, it would drastically affect many Internet protocols. In this case, "practical" means that it could be executed by an attacker with a reasonable amount of resources (one that costs a few thousand dollars and takes a few weeks might be very practical).

Privilege Escalation Attack - A privilege escalation attack is a type of network intrusion which allows the user to have an elevated access to the network which was primarily not allowed. The attacker takes the advantage of the programming errors and permits an elevated access to the network.

Probing Attack - To attempt to connect to well-known services which may be running on a system; done to see if the system exists, and potentially to identify the software it is running.

Protocol Fuzzing Attack - A testing technique used to generate valid and invalid *packets* with "random" *header field values*. The purpose is to analyze the behavior of a specific protocol by injecting unexpectedly malformed input parameter values. *Random fuzzing* is less effective, than "*smart fuzzing*" (tests based on the target specifications which requires knowledge of the building control system).

Radiation Monitoring - The process of receiving images, data, or audio from an unprotected source by listening to radiation signals.

Reflected File Download Attack (RFD) - RFD is a web attack vector that enables attackers to gain complete control over a victim's machine by forcing the browser to initiate a file download from a trusted domain using a *Windows security features bypass*. Once inside the user's computer, the attacker can use *PowerShell* to download additional payload and acquire admin rights. This attack completely *disables all warnings and files execute immediately.* See *Google Chrome Attacks.*

Relay Attack - See *Passive Keyless Entry.*

Relay Station Attack - See *Passive Keyless Entry.*

Remote Access Tool (RAT) - A piece of software that allows a remote "operator" to control a system as if he has physical access to that system. While desktop sharing and remote administration have many legal uses, *"RAT"* software is usually associated with criminal or malicious activity. *Malicious RAT* software is typically installed without the victim's knowledge, often as payload of a *Trojan horse*, and will try to hide its operation from the victim and from security software. Such tools provide an operator the following capabilities:
  1. Screen/camera capture or image control
  2. File management (download/upload/execute/etc.)
  3. Shell control (from command prompt)
  4. Computer control (power off/on/log off if remote feature is supported)
  5. Registry management (query/add/delete/modify)
  6. Hardware Destroyer (overclocker)

Remote-to-Local User (R2L) Attack - A remote-to-local cyber-attack occurs when a *cracker* who has the ability to send packets over a network (but who does not have a valid user account on the building automation system) exploits a system vulnerability to gain access as a user.

Replay Attack - A cyber-attack which involves capturing traffic sent over the network, and then re-injecting it again later, causing commands to be executed twice. Timestamps and a variety of other mechanisms are designed to prevent replay attacks.

Repudiation Attack - A repudiation attack occurs when the user denies the fact that he or she has performed a certain action or has initiated a transaction. A user can simply deny having knowledge of the transaction or communication and later claim that such transaction or communication never took place.

Resource Exhaustion Attack - A cyber-attack involving tying up limited resources on a system, making them unavailable to other users.

Resource Starvation - A condition where a computer process cannot be supported by available computer resources. Resource starvation can occur due to the lack of computer resources or the existence of multiple processes that are competing for the same computer resources.

Rogue Access Point - A rogue access point is a *wireless access point* that has been installed on a secure network without explicit authorization from a local network administrator, whether added by a well-meaning employee or by a malicious attacker. Although it is technically easy for a well-meaning employee to install a "soft access point" or an inexpensive wireless router - perhaps to make access from mobile devices easier - it is likely that they will configure this as "open", or with poor security, and potentially allow access to unauthorized parties. If an attacker installs an access point they are able to run various types of vulnerability scanners, and rather than having to be physically inside the organization, can attack remotely - perhaps from a reception area, adjacent building, or car parking lot.

Scams - Internet scams which misuse the *Microsoft* name and other general tech support scams. Scamsters phone computer users randomly and offer to fix non-existent computer problems on their computer for a fee.

Scanning Attack - Any of the following:
1. **Active Port Scanning**: Actively send network packets to enumerate all open ports of a device, including both TCP and UDP.
2. **Passive Traffic Mapping/Scanning**: Passively record network traffic. Discover ports that are normally used, without detecting open ports not actively used.
3. **Version Scanning**: Actively attempt to discover the protocol by connecting to open ports.
4. **Vulnerability Scanning**: Actively connect to a remote device and exploit known vulnerabilities.

Scareware - Scareware is a type of threat which acts as a genuine system message and guides you to download and purchase useless and potentially dangerous software. Such scareware pop-ups seem to be similar to any system messages, but actually aren't. The main purpose of the scareware is to create anxiety among the users and use that anxiety to coax them to download irrelevant software.

Scavenging Attack - Unauthorized searching through data in a system to gain knowledge of sensitive data.

Sensory Malware - *Malware* designed to hijack data collected surreptitiously from sensors on a networked device such as opportunistic images from a *smart phone*'s camera, accelerometer and geo-location information for reconnaissance purposes.

Session Hijacking Attack - A cyber-attack taking over a session that someone else established.

Shamoon Attack - An extremely destructive virus consisting of three components: a dropper, a wiper and a reporter module.
- **Dropper** is responsible for creating the required files on the system, registering a service called "TrkSvr" in order to start itself with *Windows*. It also copies itself to accessible network shares and executes itself remotely.
- **Wiper** is only activated when a hardcoded configuration date has been passed. This enables a coordinated, *"time bomb"* scenario. The module drops a legitimate and digitally signed device driver that provides low level disk access from user space. The *malware* collects file names and starts overwriting them with a JPEG image or blocks of random data. *Disttrack* finishes the computer off by wiping the *master boot record* with the same data.
- **Reporter** is responsible for sending back information to the control server. It reports the domain name, IP address and number of files overwritten.

Sideloading Attack - A term used mostly on the Internet, similar to "upload" and "download", but in reference to the process of transferring data between two local devices, in particular between a computer and a mobile device such as a mobile phone, smartphone, PDA, tablet, portable media player or e-reader.

Sinkholing Attack - The redirection of traffic from its original destination to one specified by the sinkhole owners. The altered destination is known as the sinkhole. Sinkholes can be good or bad. A *botnet sinkhole* is used to gather information about a particular botnet (that's good).

Skimming - The unauthorized use of a reader to read tags without the authorization or knowledge of the tag's owner or the individual in possession of the tag. SOURCE: SP 800-98

SMB Relay Attack - This is a cyber-attack designed to steal login credentials. Just by accessing a folder containing a malicious SCF (*Shell*

Command File), a user will unwittingly share his computer's login credentials with an attacker via *Google Chrome* and the *SMB* (*Server Message Block*) *protocol*. SCF is a shortcut file format that retrieves an icon file from the local drive. The malware instead loads the icon of an SCF file <u>from the Internet</u>. The attacker's server will ask and receive the user's login credentials because these *SMB* requests take place even if users want it or not. The *Windows OS* is built to load file icons whenever the user navigates to a folder, no questions asked, no user interaction needed.

Smishing Attack - A form of *phishing* attack that uses a cell phone text message (SMS) to lure a target to a website or prompting the target to a call a telephone number in an attempt to persuade target to reveal credit card information such as pin number. Often a *smishing* target is informed he will be charged for something unless he clicks on a link and cancels it.

Smurf Attack - A cyber-attack that spoofs the target address and sends a ping to the broadcast address for a remote network, which results in a large amount of ping replies being sent to the target.

Social Engineering Attack - Social engineering is the art and science of getting people to do something you want them to do that they might not do in the normal course of action. Instead of collecting information by technical means, intruders might also apply methods of social engineering such as impersonating individuals on the telephone, or using other persuasive means (e.g., tricking, convincing, inducing, enticing, provoking) to encourage someone to disclose information. Attackers look for information about who the target does business with, both suppliers and customers and they are particularly interested in IT support. They gather this information to better understand roles and responsibilities. They use this information to pose as someone from one of these companies. Attackers look for information such as birthdays, who was recently promoted or who just had a baby. *Hackers* do not discount any information they uncover. They will use bad relationships between IT department and other offices as a wedge to gain information.

Soft Access Point (Soft AP) - A soft access point can be set up on a Wi-Fi adapter without the need of a physical Wi-Fi router. With Windows 7 virtual Wi-Fi capabilities and Intel My Wi-Fi technology, one can easily set up a Soft AP on their machine. Once up and running, one can share the network access available on a machine to other Wi-Fi users that will connect to the soft AP. If any employee sets up a Soft AP on their machine inside the corporate premises and shares the corporate network through it, then this Soft AP behaves as Rogue Access Point.

Spam - The abuse of electronic messaging systems to indiscriminately send unsolicited bulk messages.

Spear Phishing Attack - *Phishing* attempts directed at specific individuals or companies with the sole purpose of obtaining unauthorized access to victim's sensitive data such as *network access credentials*. Attackers may gather personal information about their target to increase the probability of success. This technique is, by far, **the most successful** on the Internet today, accounting for **91%** of cyber-attacks.

Speech Recognition Cyber-Attack - An attacker crafts sounds that are difficult or impossible for humans to understand, but are interpreted as specific commands by speech-recognition systems.

Spoofing Attack - Generation of outbound network traffic pretending to be from somewhere else, typically used in a denial of service attack.

Spouseware - Typically refers to consumer surveillance malware used to monitor mobile phones or computers. Also, referred to as or *stalkerware*, since it can be used for eavesdropping on all of your spouse's texts and multimedia messages, and tracking their every move through the device's GPS. Note: Intercepting someone's private communications in the U.S. is generally illegal (one exception is a parent keeping tabs on their child).

Spyware Attack - Software that is secretly or surreptitiously installed onto an information system to gather information on individuals or organizations without their knowledge; a type of malicious code that monitors or spies on its victims. It usually remains in hiding.

SQL Injection Attack - A type of input validation attack where SQL code is inserted into database-driven application queries to manipulate the database.

SS7 Cyber-Attacks - SS7 (Signalling System 7) is a set of *telephony signaling protocols* used for data-roaming with vulnerabilities that allow attackers to listen to calls, intercept text messages, and pinpoint a device's location armed with just the target's phone number. Anyone can purchase SS7 access and send a routing request to direct a target's *SMS-based text messages* to another device, and, in the case of the bank accounts, steal any codes needed to login or greenlight money transfers (after the hackers obtained victim passwords). *NIST* no longer recommending solutions that use SMS. *Google Authenticator* is one example of a smartphone app that provides a more robust form *of two-factor authentication*, but it has other vulnerabilities.

Stack Mashing Attack - A cyber-attack using a *buffer overflow* to trick a computer into executing arbitrary code.

Stages of a Cyber-Attack -
1. **Survey** - Investigating and analyzing available information about the target in order to identify potential vulnerabilities. Attackers will use any means available to find technical, procedural or physical vulnerabilities which they can attempt to exploit. They will use open source information such as *LinkedIn* and *Facebook*, domain name management/search services, and social media. They will employ commodity toolkits and techniques, and standard network scanning tools to collect and assess any information about your organization's computers, security systems and personnel.
2. **Delivery** - Getting to the point in a system where a vulnerability can be exploited. The attacker will look to get into a position where they can exploit a vulnerability that they have identified, or they think could potentially exist. The crucial decision for the attacker is to select the best delivery path for the malicious software or commands that will enable them to breach your defenses. Examples include:
   - attempting to access an organization's online services
   - sending an email containing a link to a malicious website or an attachment which contains malicious code
   - giving an infected USB stick away at a trade fair
   - creating a false website in the hope that a user will visit
3. **Breach** - Exploiting the vulnerability/vulnerabilities to gain some form of unauthorized access. The damage will depend on the nature of the vulnerability and the exploitation method. Having done this, the attacker could pretend to be the victim and use their legitimate access rights to gain access to other systems and information. It may allow them to:
   - make changes that affect the system's operation
   - gain access to online accounts
   - achieve full control of a user's computer, tablet or smartphone
4. **Affect** - Carrying out activities within a system that achieve the attacker's goal. Depending on their motivation, the attacker may seek to explore your systems, expand their access and establish a persistent presence (a process sometimes called 'consolidation'). Taking over a

user's account usually guarantees a persistent presence. Taking over an administrator's account is an attacker's Holy Grail. With administration access to just one system, they can try to install automated scanning tools to discover more about your networks and take control of more systems. When doing this they will take great care not to trigger the system's monitoring processes and they may even disable them for a time.

Stalkerware - Typically refers to consumer surveillance malware used to monitor mobile phones or computers. Also, referred to as or *spouseware*, since it can be used for eavesdropping on all of your spouse's texts and multimedia messages, and tracking their every move through the device's *GPS*. Note: Intercepting someone's private communications in the U.S. is generally <u>illegal</u> (one exception is a parent keeping tabs on their child).

Stealth Strategy - When a virus tries to avoid detection by killing the tasks associated with antivirus software before it can detect them (for example, *Conficker*).

Stepping Stone Attack - A technique used by *cracker*s to conceal their identity and complicate their apprehension by launching attacks not from their own computer but from a chain of relay machines as intermediary compromised hosts. Each connection is made by a separate remote login so the next host in the chain can only see the identity of its immediate upper stream neighbor, and the victim only sees the identity of the last host. Even inside attackers can launder their connections through external hosts.

Stingray - An electronic device that acts like a cell phone tower and tricks cell phones into interacting with them. They can be used to track a person's location, intercept data from phones including text and voice communications, instantly drain a target's batteries completely, and disrupt service. They are also known as *ISMI Catchers* and they have a range of one to two city blocks. *Stingrays* can interfere with cell phone service and some models can be used for blanketed or targeted *denials of service*.

Stuxnet Attack - This virus targeted the S7-417 PLCs and modified its valve settings. Closing the valves at certain points in time would lead to an increase of pressure that could damage the equipment. The later version of the threat focused on the S7-315 PLCs, manipulating the spinning frequency of the rotating motors. By speeding the centrifuges up and slowing them down repeatedly, the output quality could be spoiled and the centrifuges themselves could be damaged. To hide its activity, Stuxnet executed slightly different infection routines depending on the security software installed on the target network. To avoid detection by personnel monitoring the plant, Stuxnet recorded measurement readings during normal operation and replayed those back in a loop.

Supply Chain Attack - Attacks that allow the adversary to utilize implants or other vulnerabilities inserted prior to installation in order to infiltrate data, or manipulate hardware, software, operating systems, peripherals (information technology products) or services at any point during the life cycle. For example, including a tiny *microphone* in millions of *thermostats* manufactured in a foreign country so when they are installed in sensitive rooms, they can be used to eavesdrop on conversations. SOURCE: CNSSI-4009

Sybil Cyber-Attack - A Sybil cyber-attack is the forging of multiple identities for malicious intent, named after the famous multiple personality disorder patient "*Sybil*". A spammer may create multiple web sites at different domain names that all link to each other, such as *fake blogs* (known as *spam blogs*).

SYN Flood Attack - A *denial of service* cyber-attack that sends a host more *TCP SYN packets* than the protocol can handle.

Takeover Hack - Cyber-attack of an automobile over the Internet to hijack its controls remotely such as the brakes and transmission of a vehicle on the road.

Tampering Attack - A web-based cyber-attack where certain parameters in the URL are changed without the customer's knowledge; and when the customer keys in that URL, it looks and appears exactly the same. Tampering is basically done by hackers and criminals to steal the identity and obtain illegal access to information.

Television Hacks - Computer Security firm *ReVuln* claimed it could hack *Samsung*'s newest televisions, access user settings, install malware on the TVs and any connected devices, and harvest the personal data stored on the TV. They could switch on the camera embedded in the TV and watch viewers watching the set. *Google* and *Verizon* have been reported to be developing cable TV boxes with built-in video cameras and motion sensors. If the camera detects two people on the couch, they might be delivered ads for a romantic movie, while a room full of children would see advertisements for marketing to children.

Tethering Attack - Connecting one device to another. In the context of mobile phones and tablet computers, *tethering* allows sharing the Internet connection of the phone or tablet with other devices such as laptops. Connection of the phone or tablet with other devices can be done over *wireless LAN (Wi-Fi),* over *Bluetooth* or by physical connection using a cable, for example through *USB.* Also, called a *personal hotspot.*

Tetris on the Green Hack - *Hackers* turned MIT's Green Building into a giant, playable, and multi-color Tetris game using lights in building windows. A console allowed players to move, rotate, and drop blocks.

Thermostat Hacks - Intelligent thermostats can track a user's heat and air-conditioning habits, learn user preferences, and generally surveil a location remotely. One HVAC controls manufacturer has programmed their thermostats to report temperature settings over the Internet to a company database every 12 seconds. In addition, there has been at least one instance where a thermostat produced in the Far East was manufactured so it was retasked remotely (over the Internet) to eavesdrop on sensitive conversations in a conference room.

Time Bomb Attack - Computer code that is preset to cause a later malfunction after a specific date, time, or a specific number of operations. The "Friday the 13th" computer virus is an example. This virus infects the system several days or even months before and lies dormant until the date reaches Friday the 13th.

Tiny Fragment Attack - A cyber-attack that imposes an unusually small fragment size on outgoing packets. If the fragment size is made small enough, a disallowed packet might be passed because it didn't hit a match in the filter.

Trap Door Attack - A set of instruction codes embedded in a computer operating system that permits access, while bypassing security controls.

Trojan Horse Attack - A program that causes unexpected (and usually undesirable) effects when willingly installed or run by an unsuspecting user. A *Trojan horse* is commonly disguised as a game, a utility, or an application. A person can either create or gain access to the source code of a common, frequently used program and then add code, so that the program performs a harmful function, in addition to its normal function. These programs are generally deeply buried in the code of the target program, lie dormant for a pre-selected period, and are triggered in the same manner as a *logic bomb*. A *Trojan horse* can alter, destroy, disclose data, or delete files.

Unitrix Exploit Attack - This method takes advantage of a special character in *Unicode* to reverse the order of characters in a file name, hiding the dangerous file extension in <u>the middle</u> of the file name and placing a harmless-looking fake file extension near the end of the file name. Unicode character is *U+202E: Right-to-Left Override*, and it forces programs to display text in reverse order. A file's actual name can be something like "Awesome Song uploaded by [U+202e]3pm.SCR". The special character forces Windows to display the end of the file's name in reverse, so the file's name will appear as "Awesome Song uploaded by RCS.mp3". However, it's not an *MP3* file – it's an *SCR* file and it will be executed if you double-click it.

User-to-Root (U2R) Attack - A user-to-root cyber-attack occurs when an attacker with access to a normal user account is able to exploit a system vulnerability to gain root access.

Vampire Tap - A device for physically connecting a station (e.g. a computer or printer) to a network that uses 10BASE5 cabling. This device clamps onto and "bites" into the cable (hence the vampire name), forcing a spike through a hole drilled through the outer shielding to contact the inner conductor while other spikes bite into the outer conductor. Vampire taps allow new connections to be made on a given physical cable while the cable is in use. Also, called a *piercing tap*.

Verifier Impersonation Attack - An attack where the attacker impersonates the verifier in an authentication protocol, usually to learn a password. SOURCE: SP 800-63

Virus Attack - Software buried within an existing program designed to infect a computer. A code segment that replicates by attaching copies of itself to existing executable programs. This is usually done in such a manner that the copies will be executed when the file is loaded into memory, allowing them to infect still other files, and so on. The new copy of the virus is executed when a user executes the new host program. The virus may include any additional "*payload*" that is triggered when specific conditions are met. For example, some viruses display a text string on a particular date. There are many types of viruses including variants, overwriting, resident, stealth, and polymorphic. Viruses often have damaging side effects, sometimes intentionally, sometimes not.

Vishing Attack - A type of phishing attack that uses a telephone ("v" is for voice) to obtain personal information. *Phishing* target is called directly by criminals or receives an email asking the target to call a specific phone number.

Visual Malware - A novel *Trojan Horse* app that allows a *cracker* to engage in remote reconnaissance through use of a smartphone's camera and other sensors to obtain geo-location data and its accelerometer to create a 3D map of the phone's surroundings. Using *PlaceRaider* for example, a *cracker* can download images of the physical space, study the environment and carefully construct a three-dimensional model of indoor environments to surveil the target's private home or work space. *PlaceRaider* can be used to steal virtual objects from the environment such as financial documents, information on computer monitors, and personally identifiable information.

Visual Microphones Hack - MIT researchers claim to have created an algorithm that can reconstruct sound (and even intelligible speech) with the tiny vibrations it causes on video (as small as thousandths of a pixel). When signals are averaged researchers were able to extract sound that makes sense. In the example compilation video, a bag of potato chips is filmed from 15 feet away, through sound-proof glass. Although in the reconstructed audio the words being said are not clear, the words are possible to decipher. A high-speed camera (2,000 - 6,000 frames/sec) was used, however cheap cameras could be used by taking advantage of a bug called *"rolling shutter"* that encodes information at a much higher rate than the camera's actual frame rate. This allows recovery of sound at frequencies several times higher than the frame rate of the camera.

War Dialing Attack - Dialing all the telephone numbers in a given area code to locate devices connected by a modem.

Wardriving Attack - The act of searching for Wi-Fi wireless networks by a person in a moving vehicle, using a portable computer, smartphone or *personal digital assistant* (PDA). Also, called *access point mapping*.

War Droning Attack - Use of a *cyber-drone* to search for Wi-Fi wireless networks connected to a BCS at a facility and hack into BCS networks when they are found. An aerial cyber-drone can also shut down computer systems and other nearby electronic systems from the sky through targeted emission of microwaves. *See Counter-electronics High-powered Microwave Advanced Missile Project (CHAMP).*

War Walking Attack - Just like *wardriving*, but on foot.

Water Holing Attack - Setting up a fake website or compromising a legitimate one in order to exploit visiting users.

Webcam Hack - Most webcams can be hacked. A *cracker* can watch your facility without your knowledge. This is a fairly simple hack made possible by *Trojan horse malware* called "*Blackshades*" that even a *script kiddie* can master. What's worse is a *cracker* may be able to hack into your BCS through *IP-enabled* cameras.

Whaling Attack - *Spear phishing* targeting high-profile executives, politicians and celebrities. Whaling emails are highly-personalized and appear to come from a trusted source. Once opened, the target is directed to a website that was created specifically for that individual's attack. Successful whaling targets are referred to as having been "*harpooned*".

Wireless Sensor Network (WSN) Attack - These cyber-attacks prevent sensors from detecting and transmitting data through the building automation network infrastructure.

WITCHCOVEN - *Malware* that uses profiling techniques to collect technical information on a user's computer to smartly tailor targeted operations. Cyber threat actors are building profiles of potential victims and learning about the vulnerabilities in users' computers to identify victims and tailor future infection attempts. When an unsuspecting user visits a compromised website, a small piece of inserted code—embedded in the site's *HTML* and invisible to casual visitors—quietly redirects the user's browser to a second compromised website without the user's knowledge. The second website hosts the WITCHCOVEN script, which collects technical information on the user's computer. As of early November 2015, *FireEye* identified a total of 14 websites hosting the WITCHCOVEN profiling script.

Worm Attack - A self-replicating computer program similar to a computer *virus* that harms the network and consumes bandwidth. A *worm* is a complete program that propagates itself from system to system, usually through a network or other communication facility. It is able to infect other systems and programs usually by spawning copies of itself in each computer's memory. A *worm* differs from a *virus*, in that a *virus* replicates itself, while a *worm* does not. A *worm* copies itself to a person's workstation over a network or through a host computer and then spreads to other workstations. A *worm* might duplicate itself in one computer so often that it causes the computer to crash. Sometimes written in separate segments, a *worm* is introduced surreptitiously into a host system, either for fun or with intent to damage or destroy information. It can easily take over a network, as the "Internet" worm did. Unlike a *Trojan horse*, a *worm* enters a system uninvited.

Wrapper - A type of *malware* concealed inside a legitimate software program to make it undetectable.

XcodeGhost - A counterfeit version of an *Apple* development tool, *Xcode*, downloaded by developers from third-party sources, because downloading the 4GB code from *Apple* took too long. XcodeGhost poses a privacy risk, as apps developed with XcodeGhost could be configured to record data from people's devices and sent to a remote server.

XswKit Cyber-Attack - A *fileless registry attack* malware that destroys itself upon execution and leaves no trace on the file system.

ZeroAccess Attack - A *Trojan horse bot* used to download other *malware* on an infected machine from a *botnet* mostly involved in *bitcoin mining* and click fraud, while remaining hidden on a system using rootkit techniques.

Zero Day Exploit Attack - A *worm, virus* or other cyber-threat that hits users on the same day the vulnerability is announced.

Zombie Attack - Synonym: bot.

PRESERVING FORENSIC DATA

Following are digital forensics recommendations from ICS-CERT.

Preserving forensic data is an essential aspect of any incident response plan. The forensic data acquired during the overall incident response process are critical to containing the current intrusion and improving security to defend against the next attack. An organization's network defenders should make note of the following recommendations for retention of essential forensic data:

- Keep detailed notes of all observations, including dates/times, mitigation steps taken/not taken, device logging enabled/disabled, and machine names for suspected compromised equipment. More information is generally better than less information.
- When possible, capture live system data (i.e., current network connections and open processes) prior to disconnecting a compromised machine from the network.
- Capture a forensic image of the system memory prior to powering down the system.
- When powering down a system, physically pull the plug from the wall rather than gracefully shutting down. Forensic data can be destroyed if the operating system (OS) executes a normal shut down process.
- After shutting down, capture forensic images of the host hard drives.
- Avoid running any antivirus software "after the fact" as the antivirus scan changes critical file dates and impedes discovery and analysis of suspected malicious files and timelines.
- Avoid making any changes to the OS or hardware, including updates and patches, as they might overwrite important information relevant to the analysis. Organizations should consult with trained forensic investigators for advice and assistance prior to implementing any recovery or forensic efforts.

When a compromised host is identified, it should be disconnected from the network for forensic data collection (but **not powered off**, as noted above). When all available data have been retained from the infected host, the organization should follow established internal policies for recovering the host.